THE BEST OF THE

GOOD CLEAN JOKES

BOB PHILLIPS

HARVEST HOUSE PUBLISHERS
Eugene, Oregon 97402

THE BEST OF THE GOOD CLEAN JOKES

Copyright © 1989 by Harvest House Publishers
Eugene, Oregon 97402

Phillips, Bob, 1940-
    The best of the good clean jokes / by Bob Phillips.
    Summary: A collection of jokes arranged alphabet-
    ically by topic.
    ISBN 0-89081-769-3
    1. Jokes.   2. American wit and humor.   [1. Jokes.]
    I. Title.
PN6163.P48   1989   89-32386
818'.5402—dc20   CIP
                                      AC

Printed in the United States of America.

About the Author

   With over a dozen joke books, game books, and books of colorful wisdom to his credit, BOB PHILLIPS is a master compiler of the light and humorous side of life.

   When Bob isn't out scouring the earth for humor, he directs Hume Lake Christian Camps, one of America's largest youth camping programs. He also serves as a licensed Marriage, Family, and Child Counselor.

ACHES AND PAINS

I've got so many aches and pains that if a new one comes today, it will be at least two weeks before I can worry about it.

ADAM

Sam: My daddy has a sword of Washington and a hat of Lincoln.
Bill: My father has an Adam's apple.

*   *   *

The only things Adam would recognize if he came back to earth are the jokes.

*   *   *

Eve: Adam, do you love me?
Adam: Who else?

ADVICE

Betty: Does your husband ever take advice?
Sue: Occasionally, when nobody is looking.

AFRICAN CHIEFTAIN

An African chieftain flew to the United States to visit the president. When he arrived at the airport, a host of newsmen and television cameramen met him. One of the reporters asked the chief if he had a comfortable flight.

The chief made a series of weird noises— "screech, scratch, honk, buzz, whistle, z-z-z-z-z"— and then added in perfect English, "Yes, I had a very nice flight."

Another reporter asked, "Chief, do you plan to visit the Washington Monument while you're in the area?"

The chief made the same noises—"screech, scratch, honk, buzz, whistle, z-z-z-z-z"—and then said, "Yes, and I also plan to visit the White House and the Capitol Building."

"Where did you learn to speak such flawless English?" asked the next reporter.

The chief replied, "Screech, scratch, honk, buzz, whistle, z-z-z-z-z—from the shortwave radio."

AFTER-DINNER SPEECH

Seated next to a blowhard at a United Nations

dinner was an Oriental fellow dressed in the robes of one of the Far Eastern countries.

The blowhard, attempting to make conversation, leaned over and said: "You like soupee?" The Chinese fellow nodded his head. "You like steakee?" The Oriental nodded again.

As it turned out, the guest speaker at the dinner was our Oriental friend who got up and delivered a beautiful 50-minute address on the United Nations' definition of "encouragement to self-reliance" by underdeveloped countries of the world. The speech was in flawless Oxford English.

He returned to his place at the head of the table, sat down, and turned to his dinner partner and said, "You like speechee?"

AGNOSTIC

Agnostic is Latin for ignoramus.

*   *   *

An agnostic is a person who says that he knows nothing about God and, when you agree with him, he becomes angry.

AGREEMENT

You may easily play a joke on a man who likes to argue—agree with him.

AIRLINES

A good-sized man approached the ticket counter at United Airlines and asked for a reservation from Los Angeles to New York. The clerk knew that the plane was very full with baggage and passengers.

"How much do you weigh, Sir?" asked the clerk.

"With or without clothes?" the passenger asked.

"Well," said the clerk, "how do you intend to travel?"

ALLOWANCE

Son to father: About my allowance, Pop. It's fallen below the national average for teenagers.

AMEN

The new Army recruit was given guard duty at 2 A.M. He did his best for awhile, but about 4 A.M. he went to sleep. He awakened to find the officer of the day standing before him.

Remembering the heavy penalty for being asleep on guard duty, this smart young man kept his head bowed for another moment, then looked upward and reverently said, "A-a-a-men!"

THE AMERICAN WAY

Why do we spend 5,000 dollars on a school bus to haul our children one mile, and then build a million-dollar gymnasium for them to get exercise?

AMPUTATED

Doctor: I have some good news and some bad news. Which do you want first?

Patient: Give me the bad news first.

Doctor: We amputated the wrong leg.

Patient: What is the good news?

Doctor: Your other leg won't need to be amputated after all.

ANGER

A young girl who was writing a paper for school came to her father and asked, "Dad, what is the difference between anger and exasperation?"

The father replied, "It is mostly a matter of degree. Let me show you what I mean." With that the father went to the telephone and dialed a number at random. To the man who answered the phone, he said, "Hello, is Melvin there?"

The man answered, "There is no one living here named Melvin. Why don't you learn to look up numbers before you dial them?"

"See," said the father to his daughter. "That man was not a bit happy with our call. He was probably very busy with something and we annoyed him. Now watch...."

The father dialed the number again. "Hello, is Melvin there?" asked the father.

"Now look here!" came the heated reply. "You

just called this number and I told you that there is no Melvin here! You've got a lot of nerve calling again!" The receiver slammed down hard.

The father turned to his daughter and said, "You see, that was anger. Now I'll show you what exasperation means." He again dialed the same number, and when a violent voice roared, "Hello!" the father calmly said, "Hello, this is Melvin. Have there been any calls for me?"

ANOTHER DOCTOR, PLEASE

Looking down at the sick man, the doctor decided to tell him the truth. "I feel that I should tell you: You are a very sick man. I'm sure you would want to know the facts. I don't think you have much time left. Now, is there anyone you would like to see?"

Bending down toward his patient, the doctor heard him feebly answer, "Yes."

"Who is it?"

In a slightly stronger tone, the sufferer said, "Another doctor."

ANYONE—PLEASE!

Boy: Why don't you marry me? Is there someone else?

Girl: There must be.

APATHY

The number-one problem in our country is apathy—but who cares!

APPETITE

There is one thing bigger than the overweight person's stomach: his appetite.

APPLAUSE

Applause before a speaker begins his talk is an act of faith.

Applause during the speech is an act of hope.

Applause after he has concluded is an act of charity.

APPLE

While visiting a friend who was in the hospital, I noticed several pretty nurses, each of whom was wearing a pin designed to look like an apple. I asked one nurse what the pin signified.

"Nothing," she said with a smile. "It's just to keep the doctors away."

*　　*　　*

A man traveling through the country stopped at a small fruit stand and bought some apples. When he commented they were awfully small, the farmer replied, "Yup."

The man took a bite of one of the apples and exclaimed, "Not very flavorful, either."

"That's right," said the farmer. "Lucky they're small, ain't it?"

APPROPRIATE

It was a formal banquet. The minister had just finished saying grace when a waiter spilled a bowl of steaming soup into his lap. The clergyman silently sizzled, then said in anguished tones: "Will a layman please make some appropriate remarks?"

ARGUMENT

If you really want the last word in an argument, try saying, "I guess you're right."

ARMY

The first sergeant was holding a class on combat for his company. He said, "LaHaye, what would you do if you saw 700 enemy soldiers coming at you?"

LaHaye said, "I would shoot them all with my rifle."

The sergeant asked, "On the right you see 400 enemy soldiers charging at you. What would you do?"

LaHaye said, "I would shoot them with my rifle."

The sergeant continued, "Okay! On your left, LaHaye, you notice 1,000 enemy soldiers heading straight at you. What would you do?"

LaHaye answered again, "I would shoot them all with my rifle."

The sergeant yelled, "Just a minute, LaHaye. Where are you getting all those bullets?"

The soldier smiled and said, "The same place you're getting all those enemy soldiers."

ARTHRITIS

Doctor: Say, the check you gave me for my bill came back.

Patient: So did my arthritis!

ASYLUM

Late one night in the insane asylum one inmate shouted, "I am Napoleon."

Another said, "How do you know?"

The first inmate said, "God told me."

Just then a voice from the next room shouted, "I did not."

ATHEIST

Sign on the tomb of an atheist:

HERE LIES AN ATHEIST ALL
DRESSED UP AND NO PLACE TO GO.

*   *   *

I once wanted to become an atheist, but I gave up the idea. They have no holidays.

* * *

The atheist cannot find God for the same reason that a thief cannot find a policeman.

* * *

Atheist: Do you honestly believe that Jonah spent three days and nights in the belly of a whale?

Preacher: I don't know, Sir, but when I get to heaven I'll ask him.

Atheist: But suppose he isn't in heaven?

Preacher: Then you ask him!

* * *

They have all sorts of new services today. Now they've got a dial-a-prayer service for atheists. You call a number and nobody answers.

* * *

An atheist was teasing Bill about his religious beliefs. "Come on now, Bill," he said, "Do you really believe that when you die you'll go up to heaven and fly around with wings? I understand it's not warm up there like where I'm going when I die. How in the world are you going to get your coat on over those wings?"

Bill replied, "The same way you are going to get your trousers over your tail."

*   *   *

Three atheists were trying to bother a young Baptist minister.

"I think I will move to Nevada," said the first atheist. "Only 25 percent of the people are Baptists."

"No, I think I would rather live in Colorado," said the second man, "Only ten percent of the people are Baptists."

"Better yet," said the third atheist, "is New Mexico...only five percent there are Baptist."

"I think the best place for you all is Hades," said the minister. "There are no Baptists there!"

AUDITORIUM

"Thank you for the privilege of speaking to you in this magnificent auditorium. You know the meaning of the word 'auditorium,' don't you? It is derived from two Latin words...audio, to hear, and taurus, the bull."

BABY

Getting the baby to sleep is the hardest when she is about 18 years old.

BABY BROTHER

For weeks a six-year-old lad kept telling his first-grade teacher about the baby brother or sister that was expected at his house. One day the mother allowed the boy to feel the movements of the unborn child. The six-year-old was obviously impressed, but made no comment. Furthermore, he stopped telling his teacher about the impending event. The teacher finally sat the boy on her lap and said, "Tommy, whatever has become of that baby brother or sister you were expecting at home?"

Tommy burst into tears and confessed, "I think Mommy ate it!"

BABY FOOD

I have finally figured out why babies suck their thumbs. I tried some of the baby food.

BACHELOR

Nancy: What excuse have you for not being married?

Rich: I was born that way.

BACKSEAT DRIVER

"Daddy, before you married Mommy, who told you how to drive?"

BAD BACK

When it comes to gardening, there's no better laborsaving device than a bad back.

BAD DRIVER

Did you hear about the cheerful truck driver who pulled up at a roadside café in the middle of the night for a dinner stop? Halfway through his dinner, three wild-looking motorcyclists roared up...bearded, leather-jacketed, filthy...with swastikas adorning their chests and helmets.

For no reason at all, they selected the truck driver as a target. One poured pepper over his head, another stole his apple pie, the third deliberately upset his cup of coffee. The truck driver never said one word—just arose, paid his check, and exited.

"That truck driver sure ain't much of a fighter," sneered one of the invaders. The girl behind the counter, peering out into the night, added, "He doesn't seem to be much of a driver either. He just ran his truck right over three motorcycles."

BAD LANGUAGE

One day an elderly lady was shocked by the language used by two men repairing telephone wires near her home. She even wrote a letter to the company complaining about the matter. The foreman was ordered to report the happening to his superior. "Me and Joe Wilson were on this job," he reported. "I was up on the telephone pole and I accidentally let hot lead fall on Joe and it went down his neck. Then he called up to me, 'You really must be more careful, Harry.' "

BAD NEWS

Good news: All of you slaves on the galley are going to get an extra-special ration of rum with the noon meal.

Bad news: After lunch, the captain wants to go waterskiing.

BAD SITUATIONS

Talk about bad situations...just think about:

A screen door on a submarine.
A stowaway on a kamikaze plane.
A teenager who parks in a dark alley with his girl and his horn gets stuck.
A soup sandwich.
One who ejects from a helicopter.
A Hindu snake charmer with a deaf cobra.

BALD

If a man is bald in front, he's a thinker. If he's bald in the back, he's a lover. If he's bald in front and back, he thinks he's a lover.

BALD-HEADED

At a certain time of life, a man's hair begins to grow inward. If it strikes gray matter, it turns gray. If it doesn't strike anything, it disappears.

*   *   *

Today's toupees really fool people, but only those people who wear them.

BANANA

Man (to woman on train): That is the ugliest baby I have ever seen!

Woman: Conductor! Conductor! This man has just insulted my baby!

Conductor: Now, Madam, don't get mad. I'll get a drink of water for you and a banana for your baby.

BANK

Credit manager: Do you have any money in the bank?

Loan applicant: Certainly.

Credit manager: How much?

Loan applicant: I don't know. I haven't shaken it lately.

BAPTISTS

"Some people say the Baptist denomination started with John the Baptist, but is was much earlier than that," said a great Baptist leader as he spoke to a large gathering of Baptist ministers. "In fact, it started way over in the Old Testament. In the thirteenth chapter of Genesis, it says Lot said to Abraham, 'You go your way and I'll go mine.' That's when the Baptists began."

*   *   *

Q. When you have 50 people all of different opinions, what do you have?
A. A Baptist church.

BARE FEET

Q. Do you know what happened to the pregnant lady who got frightened by the bear at the zoo?
A. Her baby was born with bare feet!

BARK

A sportsman went to a hunting lodge and bagged a record number of birds, aided by a dog named Salesman. Next year he returned and asked for Salesman again. "The hound ain't no durn good now," the handler said.

"What happened!" cried the sportsman. "Was he injured?"

"No. Some fool came down here and called him 'Sales Manager' all week instead of Salesman. Now all he does is sit on his tail and bark."

BASEBALL

Baseball is talked about a great deal in the Bible: In the big inning, Eve stole first—Adam stole second—Gideon rattled the pitchers—Goliath was put out by David—and the Prodigal Son made a home run.

BEANS AGAIN

Husband: Beans again!
Wife: I don't understand it. You liked beans on Monday, Tuesday, and Wednesday, and now all of a sudden you don't like beans.

BEAUTIFUL

My wife is just as beautiful today as when I married her 20 years ago...of course, it takes her longer.

BEAUTY SHOP

"My wife spent four hours in the beauty shop the other day."
"Boy, that's a long time."
"Yeah, and that was just for the estimate!"

BEHAVIOR

Father: Do you think it will improve Junior's behavior if we buy him a bicycle?

Mother: No, but it'll spread his behavior over a wider area.

BESTSELLER

If you think no evil, see no evil, and hear no evil, the chances are that you'll never write a bestselling novel.

BETTER TREATMENT

After a family disturbance, one of the little boys closed his bedtime prayer by saying, "And please don't give my dad any more children.... He don't know how to treat those he's got now."

BIFOCALS

The five "B's" of old age are: bifocals...bunions...bridges...bulges...and baldness.

BIG BUCKS

The three sons of a lawyer, a doctor, and a minister were talking about how much money their fathers made.

The lawyer's son said, "My father goes into court on a case and often comes home with as much as 1,500 dollars."

The doctor's son said, "My father performs an operation and earns as much as 2,000 dollars for it."

The minister's son, determined not to be outdone, said, "That's nothing. My father preaches for just 20 minutes on Sunday morning, and it takes four men to carry the money."

THE BIG HAND

Pilot: Control tower, what time is it?

Control tower: What airline is this?

Pilot: What difference does that make?

Control tower: If it is United Airlines, it is 6:00 P.M.; if it is TWA, it is 1800 hours; if it is Ozark, the big hand is on the..."

BIG JOHN

A very small, sickly-looking man was hired as a bartender. The saloon owner gave him a word of warning: "Drop everything and run for your life if ever you hear that Big John is on his way to town." The man worked several months without any problems.

Then one day a cowhand rushed in shouting, "Big John is a'comin'," and knocked the small bartender on the floor in his hurry to get out. Before the bartender had a chance to recover, a giant of a man with a black bushy beard rode into the saloon through the swinging doors on the back of a buffalo, and using a rattlesnake for a whip. The man tore the doors off their hinges, knocked over tables, and flung the snake into the corner. He then took his massive fist and split the bar in half as he asked for a drink. The bartender nervously pushed a bottle at the man. He bit off the top of the bottle with his teeth and downed the contents in one gulp, and turned to leave. Seeing that he wasn't hurting anyone, the bartender asked the man if he would like another drink. "I ain't got no time," the man roared. "Big John is a'comin' to town."

BIG LIAR

Stranger: Catch any fish?

Fisherman: Did I! I took 30 out of this stream this morning.

Stranger: Do you know who I am? I'm the game warden.

Fisherman: Do you know who I am? I'm the biggest liar in the country.

BIG STORY

"I'm really worried."

"Why?"

"Well, my wife read *A Tale of Two Cities* and we had twins. Later she read *The Three Musketeers* and we had triplets. Now she is reading *Birth of a Nation*!"

BIGAMY

Son: Dad, does bigamy mean that a man has one wife too many?

Dad: Not necessarily, Son. A man can have one wife too many and still not be a bigamist.

BIGGER PIECE

Speaking about marriages of high school kids, one elderly gent of 20 swore he attended a wedding ceremony where the bridegroom wept for two hours. It seems the bride got a bigger piece of cake than he did.

BIRD LEGS

A young college student had stayed up all night studying for his zoology test the next day. As he entered the classroom, he saw ten stands with ten birds on them with a sack over each bird and only the legs showing. He sat right on the front row because he wanted to do the best job possible. The professor announced that the test would be to look at each set of bird legs and give the common name, habitat, genus, species, etc.

The student looked at each set of bird legs. They all looked the same to him. He began to get upset. He had stayed up all night studying, and now had to identify birds by their legs. The more he thought about it, the madder he got. Finally, he could stand it no longer. He went up to the professor's desk and said, "What a stupid test! How could anyone tell the difference between birds by looking at their legs?" With that the student threw his test on the professor's desk and walked out the door.

The professor was surprised. The class was so big that he didn't know every student's name, so as the student reached the door the professor called, "Mister, what's your name?"

The enraged student pulled up his pant legs and said, "You guess, buddy! You guess!"

BIRTHSTONE

Son: Dad, this magazine article says that my birthstone is the ruby. What is yours?

Father: The grindstone.

BIRTHDAY

Husband to wife: How do you expect me to remember your birthday when you never look any older?

BIRTHMARK

He has a small birthmark on his head...his brain.

BITTER

"I have a bitter taste in my mouth."

"Been biting your tongue?"

BLABBERMOUTH

To guests he is the gracious host,
To children three he is "the most,"
To loving wife the perfect mate,
To fellow workers he's "just great!"

How SAD then that a humble friend
Upon his promise can't depend,
From east to west, from north to south,
His name? You guessed it! BLABBERMOUTH!

BLAME

To err is human; to blame it on the other guy is even more human.

BLANK

A new preacher had just begun his sermon. He was a little nervous, and about ten minutes into the talk his mind went blank. He remembered what they had taught him in seminary to do when a situation like this would arise—repeat your last point. Often this would help you remember what is coming next. So he thought he would give it a try.

"Behold, I come quickly," he said. Still his mind was blank. He thought he would try it again. "Behold I come quickly." Still nothing.

He tried it one more time with such force that he fell forward, knocking the pulpit to one side, tripping over a flowerpot, and falling into the lap of a little old lady in the front row.

The young preacher apologized and tried to explain what happened.

"That's all right, young man," said the little old lady. "It was my fault. I should have gotten out of the way. You told me three times you were coming!"

BLIND

Two men were riding on a train for the first time. They brought bananas for lunch. Just as one of them bit into his banana, the train entered a tunnel.

First man: Did you take a bite of your banana?
Second man: No.
First man: Well, don't! I did and went blind!

BLUE RIBBON

A minister from the city was filling the pulpit in a small farm community. After his sermon he was invited over to the house of one of the members for lunch. In the course of the conversation, he mentioned with pride that his son had won first prize in the 100-yard dash.

"I know just how you must feel," declared the member understandingly. "I remember how pleased I was last year when our pig got the blue ribbon at the fair."

BLUFF

Boy: If you refuse to be mine, I'll hurl myself off that 500-foot cliff over there.

Girl: That's a lot of bluff.

BLUNDER

Mark Twain was once asked the difference between a mistake and a blunder. He explained it this way: "If you walk into a restaurant and walk out with someone's silk umbrella and leave your own cotton one, that is a mistake. But if you pick up someone's cotton umbrella and leave your own silk one, that's a blunder."

THE BOOK OF PARABLES

Recently I interviewed a _____ (teacher, student, or whoever) from _____ (name of church, school, or organization you are speaking to) and asked (him/her) some Bible questions. I could tell that they had really learned a great deal, so I asked them what their favorite book of the Bible was. They said, "The New Testament." I replied, "What part of the New Testament?" They said, "Oh, by far, I love the Book of Parables best." I asked, "Would you kindly relate one of those parables to me?"

They said, "Once upon a time, a man went from Jerusalem to Jericho and fell among thieves. The thieves threw him into the weeds, and the weeds grew up and choked that man. He then went on and met the Queen of Sheba and she gave that man a thousand talents of gold and silver and a hundred changes of raiment. He then got in his chariot and drove furiously to the Red Sea. When he got there, the waters parted and he drove to the other side.

"On the other side he drove under a big olive tree and got his hair caught on a limb and was left hanging there. He hung there many days and many nights and the ravens brought him food to eat and water to drink. One night while he was hanging there asleep his wife Delilah came along and cut off his hair, and he dropped and fell on stony ground. The children of a nearby city came out and said, 'Go up, thou baldhead, go up, thou baldhead.' And the man cursed the children and two she bears came out of the woods and tore up the children.

"Then it began to rain and it rained for 40 days and 40 nights. And he went and hid himself in a cave. Later he went out and met a man and said, 'Come and take supper with me.' But the man replied, 'I cannot come for I have married a wife.' So he went out into the highways and byways and compelled them to come in, but they would not heed his call.

"He then went on to Jericho and blew his trumpet seven times and the city walls came tumbling down. As he walked by one of the damaged buildings in the city, he saw Queen Jezebel sitting high up in a window and when she saw him she laughed and made fun of him. The man grew furious and said, 'Toss her down.' And they did. Then he said, 'Toss her down again.' And they did. They threw her down seventy times seven. And the fragments they gathered up were 12 baskets full. The question now is...'Whose wife will she be on the day of resurrection?' "

BOOKWORM

Martha: Is your husband a bookworm?
Roberta: No, just an ordinary one.

BORE

A bore is someone who goes on talking while you're interrupting.

* * *

Mark Twain was once trapped by a bore who lectured to him about the hereafter: "Do you realize that every time I exhale, some poor soul leaves this world and passes on to the great beyond?"
"Really? Why don't you try chewing cloves?"

BRAIN FOOD

Husband: I hear that fish is brain food.
Wife: You had better eat a whale.

* * *

Student: I hear that fish is brain food.
Roommate: Yeah, I eat it all the time.
Student: Well, there goes another theory.

BRAINS

"How long can a man live without brains?"
"I don't know. How old are you?"

*   *   *

Father: Don't you think our son gets all his brains from me?
Mother: Probably. I still have all mine.

*   *   *

Don: She's a bright girl...she has brains enough for two.
Art: Then she's just the girl for you.

BREATH

Husband: This report says that every time I breathe, three Chinese people die.
Wife: That doesn't surprise me. You've got to stop eating so much garlic.

*   *   *

"Oh, I can't catch my breath."
"With your breath you should be thankful!"

BRIGHT IDEA

An old Chinaman was eating too much rice, especially since he was too frail to work. Because the man had become a burden, the father of the home—the old Chinaman's son—determined to get rid of him. He put him in a wheelbarrow, then started up the mountain. The little eight-year-old grandson went along. He was full of questions. His father explained that the grandfather was old and useless and the only thing they could do was to take him up the mountain and leave him to die. Then the grandson had a bright idea. "I'm glad you brought me along, Father, because when you're old, I'll know where to take you."

BUBBLE

Is that your head, or did your body blow a bubble?

BUFFALO

She has early-American features...she looks like a buffalo.

BUM

She refuses to give him a divorce. She says, "I've suffered with the bum for 15 years, and now I should make him happy?"

BURGLAR

Jan: Wake up, John. There's a burglar going through your pants pockets.

John: Oh, you two just fight it out between yourselves.

BUSY

No matter how busy people are, they are never too busy to stop and talk about how busy they are.

CAIN

Heckler: Who was Cain's wife?

Preacher: I respect any seeker of knowledge, but I want to warn you, young man, don't risk being lost to salvation by too much inquiring after other men's wives.

CAKE

Wife: Darling, you know that cake you asked me to bake for you? Well, the dog ate it.

Husband: That's okay, dear; don't cry. I'll buy you another dog.

CAMEL

Q. What do you call a camel without a hump?
A. Humphrey.

*   *   *

Noah was standing at the gangplank checking off the pairs of animals when he saw three camels trying to get on board.

"Wait a minute!" said Noah. "Two each is the limit. One of you will have to stay behind."

"It won't be me," said the first camel. "I'm the camel whose back is broken by the last straw."

"I'm the one people swallow while straining at a gnat," said the second.

"I," said the third, "am the one that shall pass through the eye of a needle sooner than a rich man shall enter heaven."

"Come on in," said Noah. "The world is going to need all of you."

CAN YOU TOP THIS?

The following conversation was overheard at a party attended by high-society people:

"My ancestry goes all the way back to Alexander the Great," said one lady. She then turned to a second lady and said, "And how far does your family go back?"

"I don't know," was the reply. "All of our records were lost in the Flood."

CANCER

"Would you like a cigarette?"
"No, thank you. I think I already have cancer!"

CAN'T SWIM

A hunter shot a duck and it fell into the lake. Quickly, he commanded his dog—a dog he had never worked before—to retrieve. The hound ran to the edge of the water, sniffed, and walked out on the lake. The hunter was amazed. He shot another duck; it, too, fell into the lake. Again the hound walked out on the water to retrieve the duck before it sank. At last, the hunter thought, he had something to show that friend of his who never let anything get to him. The next day the hunter suggested to his friend that they go do a little duck shooting. His friend shot a duck, and it fell into the lake. The dog walked across the water to retrieve it and drop it at the shooter's feet.

The hunter asked his friend, "What do you think of my bird dog? Didn't you notice anything special about my dog?"

"I noticed one thing. He can't swim."

CAR

Fifteen-year-old Fred: Dad, the Bible says that if you don't let me have the car, you hate me.

Dad: Where does it say that?

Son: Proverbs 13:24: "He that spareth his 'rod' hateth his son."

CAR KEYS

The other day I was playing golf and saw an

unusual thing. A golfer became so mad that he threw his brand-new set of golf clubs into the lake. A few minutes later he came back, waded into the lake, and retrieved his clubs. He proceeded to take his car keys out of the bag and then threw the clubs back into the water.

CAR SICKNESS

The feeling you get every month when the payment is due.

CAREER

Father pacing floor with a wailing baby in his arms as his wife lies snug in bed: "Nobody ever asks me how I manage to combine marriage and a career."

CAT FOOD

A butcher was waiting on one woman when a second woman ran into the shop. "Quick," the second woman said to the butcher, "give me a pound of cat food, will you?" Then she turned to the woman who had been ahead of her at the counter. "I hope you don't mind my butting in ahead of you," she said.

"No," said the first woman, "not if you're that hungry."

CATCH THE BUS

There's a bus leaving in ten minutes. Be under it!

CEMENT

"You heard my speech, Professor. Do you think it would improve my delivery if I followed the example of Demosthenes and practiced my diction and elocution with pebbles and marbles in my mouth?"

"I would recommend quick-dry cement."

CEMETERY PLOT

"What did you give your wife for Christmas last year?"

"A cemetery plot!"

"What are you going to give her this year?"

"Nothing. She didn't use last year's gift!"

CHALK

(The following is a story that can be told about a clergyman or a friend.)

One day I had a dream about my friend _____. I dreamed that he died and went to heaven. But in the dream the way to heaven was to climb a ladder. And as anyone climbed the ladder, he was supposed to take a piece of chalk and make a mark on each rung for each sin he had committed.

As I looked in my dream I saw _____ coming down the ladder. I asked him what he was doing. He said he was coming down for more chalk.

CHALLENGE

Counsel: Do you wish to challenge any of the jury?

Prisoner: Well, I think I could lick that little fellow on this end.

CHANGE THE ROPE

An old European monastery is perched high on a 500-foot cliff. Visitors ride up in a big basket, pulled to the top with a ragged old rope.

Halfway up, a passenger nervously asked: "How often do you change the rope?"

The monk in charge replied: "Whenever the old one breaks."

CHAPPED

Harry: Please give me a kiss.

Carrie: My lips are chapped.

Harry: Well, one more chap won't hurt them.

CHAPPED LIPS

Q. What's worse than a giraffe with a sore throat?

A. A hippopotamus with chapped lips.

CHATTERBOX

Mark Twain's hostess at the opera had chattered so much that no one in her box had been able to enjoy the singing. At the end of the performance she said, "Mr. Clemens, I want you to be my guest next Friday night, too. They are going to give Tosca then."

"Charmed," said Twain. "I've never heard you in that."

CHAUVINISM

HOW TO TELL A BUSINESSMAN FROM A BUSINESSWOMAN:

A businessman is dynamic; a businesswoman is aggressive.

He is good on details; she is picky.

He loses his temper; she is crabby.

He's a go-getter; she is pushy.

When he's depressed, everyone tiptoes past his office; when she is moody, it must be her time of the month.

He follows through; she doesn't know when to quit.

He's confident; she is stuck-up.

He stands firm; she's hard as nails.

He has the courage of his convictions; she is
   stubborn.

He is a man of the world; she's been around.

He can handle his liquor; she's a lush.

He isn't afraid to say what he thinks; she's
   mouthy.

He's human; she's emotional.

He exercises authority diligently; she is
   power-mad.

He is closemouthed; she is secretive.

He can make quick decisions; she's impulsive.

He runs a tight ship; she's hard to work for.

CHECK

A young college student wrote home to his
family: "Dear Mom and Dad, I haven't heard from
you in nearly a month. Please send a check so I'll
know you're all right."

CHEERFUL GIVER

Hoping to develop his son's character, a father
once gave his son a penny and a quarter as he was
leaving for Sunday school. "Now Bill, you put
whichever one you want in the offering plate," he
said.

When the boy returned, his father asked which
coin he had given. Bill answered, "Well, just before
they sent around the plate the preacher said, 'The
Lord loveth a cheerful giver,' and I knew I could

give the penny a lot more cheerfully than I could
give the quarter, so I gave the penny."

CHESS

A man dropped in to pay a friend an unexpected
visit, and was amazed to find him playing chess
with a dog. The man watched in silence for a few
minutes, then burst out with, "That's the most
incredible dog I ever saw in my life!"

"Oh, he isn't so smart," the friend answered.
"I've beaten him three games out of four."

CHEW WITH YOUR MOUTH CLOSED

"He's such a great speaker. I'd rather hear him
speak than eat."

"Me, too. I sat at the head table with him. I've
heard him eat."

THE CHIEF HOG

A church secretary answered the phone and
heard the caller say, "I want to talk to the chief hog
of the trough."

"Sir," she replied, "that is no way to talk about
the Reverend. He is the pastor of this church."

"Sorry, Lady," he said, "I just wanted to donate
$100,000 to the church."

Quickly she said, "Just a minute. Here comes the
big fat pig now."

CHILDREN

The trouble with your children is that when they're not being a lump in your throat, they're being a pain in your neck.

* * *

"Billy, get your little brother's hat out of that mud puddle."
"I can't, Ma. He's got it strapped too tight under his chin."

* * *

The greatest aid to adult education is children.

* * *

Father: Why are you always at the bottom of your class?
Dennis: It doesn't make any difference. They teach the same thing at both ends.

* * *

Mother: Suzie, what have you been doing this morning while I was working in the kitchen?
Suzie: I was playing postman.
Mother: How could you play postman when you don't have any letters?

Suzie: I was looking through your trunk in the garage and found a packet of letters tied with a nice ribbon, and I posted one in everyone's mailbox on the block.

CHINA

"What do you think of Red China?" one lady asked another during a luncheon on world affairs.

"Oh, I don't know," replied the other lady. "I guess it would be all right if you used it on a yellow tablecloth."

CHIPS

A man arrested for gambling came before the judge. "We weren't playing for money," he explained to the judge. "We were just playing for chips."

"Chips are just the same as money," the judge sternly replied. "I fine you 15 dollars."

The defendant looked sad, then slowly reached into his pocket and handed the judge three blue chips.

CHLOROFORM

Boy: What would I have to give you for one little kiss?

Girl: Chloroform!

CHOIR

The choir soloist was practicing in the church with all the windows open. When she stepped outside for a breath of fresh air, she noticed the gardener working in the flower bed. "How did you like my execution?" the soloist asked.

The gardener looked up and said, "I'm in favor of it."

CHOP

A lady senator was trying to speak to an audience of farmers from her area. A man who opposed her stood up and challenged her. "Why should you represent us? You don't come from a farm. I'd even like to know if you know how many toes a pig has."

Quick as a flash the lady senator replied, "Sir, why don't you take off your shoes and count them?"

CHOP TO THE EGO

"Whatever I say goes."

"Then why don't you talk about yourself for awhile?"

CHRISTMAS

There's nothing like the Christmas season to put a little bounce in your checks.

*   *   *

A famous writer once sent Christmas cards containing nothing but 25 letters of the alphabet. When some of his friends admitted that they had failed to understand his message, he pointed to the card and said, "Look! No L!"

CHURCH

Church...A place where you encounter nodding acquaintances.

*   *   *

A visiting pastor at a country church asked one of the farmers if he could use his barn to get away where it was quiet and study for his message. After several hours of study, the pastor left the barn for a walk. When he came back, he discovered that the cow had eaten all of his sermon notes. The next day the farmer complained to the pastor that his cow had gone dry.

*   *   *

"If absence makes the heart grow fonder," said a minister, "a lot of folks must love our church."

* * *

Wife: Did you see that hat Mrs. Jones wore to church?
Husband: No!
Wife: Did you see the new dress Mrs. Smith had on?
Husband: No!
Wife: A lot of good it does you to go to church!

CHURCH MEMBERS

First pastor: I hear you had a revival.
Second pastor: Yes, we did.
First pastor: How many additions did you have?
Second pastor: We didn't have any additions but we had some blessed subtractions.

CIGAR

"Will my smoking this cigar bother you?"
"Not if my getting sick won't bother you!"

CIVILIZED

Bob was exceptionally bald. Bill was prematurely gray. One day these two met on the street and Bob said, "Bill, you are certainly getting gray."

"Yes, said Bill, "but I'd rather be gray than bald like you, especially since I learned the cause of both. Scientists claim that the roots of the hair grow in deeply and when they strike something gray the hair naturally turns the same color. If the roots strike nothing, the hair falls out."

"On the other hand," said Bob, "historians have learned that all barbarians have hair, which seems to prove that the less hair you have, the more civilized you are."

CLEAN IT UP

Q. If a man crosses the ocean twice without taking a bath, what is he called?

A. A dirty double-crosser.

CLERGYMAN

Two men named Richard Hanson lived near each other in the same community. One was a minister and the other was a businessman. The minister passed away at about the same time as the businessman went on a trip to Florida.

When the businessman arrived in Florida, he sent a telegram to his wife informing her of his safe arrival. Unfortunately, the message was delivered in error to the wife of the recently deceased minister.

The telegram read: ARRIVED SAFELY; HEAT HERE TERRIFIC.

CLOTHES

Teenager Mary was in tears the other night

because she had nothing to wear for her date. All her sweatshirts were in the wash.

COACH

A coach was being congratulated on having a lifetime contract. "I guess it's all right," he said. "But I remember another guy with a lifetime contract. Had a bad year, and the president called him in, pronounced him dead, and fired him."

COBWEB

"I heard about an artist who painted a cobweb on the ceiling so realistically that the maid spent hours trying to get it down."

"Sorry, I don't believe it."

"Why not? Artists have been known to do such things."

"Yes, but maids haven't."

COLD CUT

Buck: Were you ever married?

Glen: Yeah, but my wife ran away.

Buck: How did it happen?

Glen: She ran away when I was taking a bath.

Buck: I'll bet she waited years for the opportunity.

COLD GROUND

Was the ground cold when you crawled out this morning?

COLLEGE

Q. What's the difference between a mental institution and a college?
A. In the mental institution you must show improvement to get out.

COLLEGE CHEER

The check from home.

COLONEL SANDERS

A farmer vows he increased egg production by putting this sign in the henhouse: "An egg a day keeps Colonel Sanders away."

COMEDIAN

A person who has a good memory for old jokes.

COMFORTABLE

The quickest way for a parent to get a child's attention is to sit down and look comfortable.

COMMENCE VACATION

A traveling salesman was held up in the West by a storm and flood. He wired his office in New York: DELAYED BY STORM. SEND INSTRUCTIONS.

His boss wired back: COMMENCE VACATION IMMEDIATELY.

COMMITTEE

A certain congregation was about to erect a new church edifice. The building committee, in consecutive meetings, passed the following resolutions:

1. We shall build a new church.

2. The new building is to be located on the site of the old one.

3. The material in the old building is to be used in the new one.

4. We shall continue to use the old building until the new one is completed.

COMPETITION

Two barber shops were in red-hot competition. One put up a sign advertising haircuts for 75 cents. His competitor put up one that read, "We repair 75-cent haircuts."

COMPLAINT

Waiter: We haven't had a complaint in 25 years.
Customer: No wonder. The customers all starve to death before they are served.

*   *   *

Customer in restaurant: I'll have some raw oysters, not too small, not too salty, not too fat. They must be cold, and I want them quickly!
Waiter: Yes, Sir. With or without pearls?

COMPLETE PROTECTION

Watching the television news, we find that our highways aren't safe, our streets aren't safe, our parks aren't safe...but under our arms we've got complete protection.

COMPLIMENT

Whenever a man's friends begin to compliment him about looking young, he may be sure that they think he is growing old—Washington Irving.

COMPUTER

If computers get too powerful, we can organize them into committees. That'll do them in.

CONCENTRATE

Member: Pastor, how did you get that cut on your face?

Pastor: I was thinking about my sermon this morning and wasn't concentrating on what I was doing and cut myself while shaving.

Member: That's too bad! Next time you had better concentrate on your shaving and cut your sermon!

CONCLUSION

He needs no introduction. What he needs is a conclusion.

* * *

The troops were being taught to jump from a plane:

"What if my parachute doesn't open?" asked one rookie.

"That," said the instructor, "is known as jumping to a conclusion."

* * *

Jumping at conclusions is not half as much exercise as digging for facts.

CONCUSSION

A doctor, appearing as an expert witness on behalf of a man injured in a car accident, was being badgered by an overbearing attorney.

"You say, Doctor, that you're familiar with the symptoms of a brain concussion?"

"That's correct," replied the doctor.

"Well tell me, Doctor," continued the attorney, "if you and I were riding in a car and another car struck us and our heads bumped together, is it your opinion that we would suffer a concussion?"

"It's my opinion," replied the doctor, "that I would and you wouldn't."

CONFIDENCE

A burglar, needing money to pay his income taxes, decided to burgle the safe in a store. On the safe door he was very pleased to find a note reading: "Please don't use dynamite. The safe is not locked. Just turn the knob." He did so. Instantly a heavy sandbag fell on him, the entire premises were floodlighted, and alarms started clanging. As the police carried him out on a stretcher, he was heard moaning: "My confidence in human nature has been rudely shaken."

CONSCIENCE

Mark Twain used to tell the story of how he once

stole a watermelon from a cart when the owner was not looking. He carried the melon to a secret spot, sat down, and was just about to bite into the melon when he realized that he should not do that. It just wasn't right.

So he got up, took the watermelon back, replaced it on the cart, and took a ripe one.

CONSULTATION

A medical term meaning "share the wealth."

COOK

Bride: The two best things I cook are meat loaf and apple dumplings.
Groom: Well, which is this?

COOKIES

Wife: I baked two kinds of cookies today. Would you like to take your pick?
Husband: No thanks. I'll use my hammer.

COUGHING

People who cough incessantly never seem to go to a doctor—they go to banquets, concerts, and church.

COURAGE

Someday I would like to see a waiter with enough courage to lay the check faceup on the table.

COVER-UP

A bald man's retort: "In the beginning God created all men bald; later He became ashamed of some and covered them up with hair."

CRANE

She looks like she had her face lifted and the crane broke.

CRAZY

The psychiatrist said sternly to the patient: "If you think you're walking out of here cured after only three sessions, you're crazy."

CRAZY BONE

Husband: Ouch! I bumped my crazy bone.
Wife: Oh well, comb your hair right and the bump won't show.

CREDIT

Glen: Are you still living within your income?

Rich: No. It's all I can do to live within my credit.

* * *

The man had barely paid off the mortgage on his house when he mortgaged it again to buy a car and, not long after, he borrowed to build a garage. His banker hesitated and said, "If I do make this new loan, how will you buy gas for the car?"

"It seems to me," replied the borrower curtly, "that a fellow who owns a big house, a car, and a garage should be able to get credit for gasoline."

CREEP

He's the kind of guy that can really creep into your heart and mind. In fact, you'll never meet a bigger creep!

CREW CUT

I couldn't stand my boy's long hair any longer, so I dragged him with me to the barbershop and ordered, "Give him a crew cut." The barber did just that and, so help me, I found I'd been bringing up somebody else's son!

CRIB

One night a wife found her husband standing over their baby's crib. Silently she watched him. As he stood looking down at the sleeping infant, she saw on his face a mixture of emotions: disbelief, doubt, delight, amazement, enchantment, skepticism.

Touched by this unusual display and the deep emotions it aroused, with eyes glistening she slipped her arm around her husband.

"A penny for your thoughts," she said.

"It's amazing!" her replied. "I just can't see how anybody can make a crib like that for only $46.50."

CRIME

We don't seem to be able to check crime, so why not legalize it and then tax it out of business?—Will Rogers.

CROSSWORD PUZZLE

Did you hear about the crossword puzzle addict who died and was buried six feet down and three feet across?

CUPID

Cupid's dart hurt more coming out than going in.

CURIOSITY

A sharp nose indicates curiosity. A flattened nose indicates too much curiosity.

CUT OFF YOUR HEAD

A sure-fire way to lose ten ugly pounds: Cut off your head!

CYCLONE

A Kansas cyclone hit a farmhouse just before dawn one morning. It lifted the roof off, picked up the beds on which the farmer and his wife slept, and set them down gently in the next county.

The wife began to cry.

"Don't be scared, Mary," her husband said. "We're not hurt."

Mary continued to cry. "I'm not scared," she responded between sobs. "I'm happy 'cause this is the first time in 14 years we've been out together."

DAMP

Pam: Why was your letter so damp?
Rosie: Postage due, I guess.

DANCE

Rod: I'm through with that girl.

Doug: Oh, why?

Rod: She asked me if I danced.

Doug: Well, what's wrong with that?

Rod: I was dancing with her when she asked me.

DARLING

A sorely-pressed newlywed sought valiantly to console his little bride, who sprawled, dissolved in tears, on the chaise lounge. "Darling," he implored, "believe me. I never said you were a terrible cook. I merely pointed out that our garbage disposal has developed an ulcer."

DEACON

Pastor: Say, Deacon, a mule died out in the front of the church.

Deacon: Well, it's the job of you ministers to look after the dead. Why tell me?

Pastor: You're right; it is my job. But we always notify the next of kin.

DEAD IN CHRIST

One pastor said that his church people would be the first to go up in the rapture. He gave his reason: "The Bible says, 'The dead in Christ shall rise first.'"

DEAD OR ALIVE

"When I went out with Fred, I had to slap his face five times."

"Was he that fresh?"

"No! I thought he was dead!"

DEAF

Stewardess: I'm sorry, Mr. Jones, but we left your wife behind in Chicago.

Man: Thank goodness! For a moment there I thought I was going deaf!

DEAF AND DUMB

Hokum: What do you mean by telling everyone I am deaf and dumb?

Yokum: That's not true. I never said you were deaf.

DEAR JOHN

One of Joe's bunk mates broke up with his girlfriend. The girlfriend wrote demanding that he return her photograph immediately. The soldier borrowed a collection of several pictures of various girls and sent them to his ex-sweetheart with her photo tucked in among them. He enclosed a note:

"Dear Mildred, pick out yours. I have forgotten what you look like."

DECEIVE

PK: She said I'm interesting, brave, and intelligent.

Bob: You should never go steady with a girl who deceives you from the very start.

DECISIONS

Did you hear about the parents who sent their young son to camp to learn to make decisions of his own? He did—the second day there he decided to come home.

DEEP WATER

When you are in deep water, it's a good idea to keep your mouth shut.

DEFENDANT

"You have known the defendant how long?"

"Twelve years."

"Tell the court whether you think he is the type of man who would steal this money or not."

"How much was it?"

DEMOCRATS

The Southern father was introducing his family of boys to a visiting governor.

"Thirteen boys," exclaimed the governor. "And all Democrats, I suppose."

"All but one," said the father proudly. "They're all Democrats but Willie, the little rascal. He got to readin'."

DEPRESSION

Three causes of housewife depression: ABC...NBC...CBS.

DESPERATION

The robber stuck a gun in the man's back, but the man turned suddenly, applied a judo grip, and flung the robber across the alley. Then he pounced on the robber and began to wipe him out. He blackened his eyes, broke his jaw, fractured his ribs, and broke both his arms. Finally the crook cried in desperation, "Hey Mister, ain't you never gonna call a cop?"

DEVIL

A man was going to attend a Halloween party dressed in a costume of the devil. On his way it began to rain, so he darted into a church where a revival meeting was in progress.

At the sight of his devil's costume, people began to scatter through the doors and windows.

One lady got her coat sleeve caught on the arm of one of the seats and, as the man came closer, she pleaded, "Satan, I've been a member of this church for 20 years, but I've really been on your side all the time."

DIED

Pastor: Isn't this a beautiful church? Here is a plaque for the men who died in the service.
Man: Which one—morning or evening?

DIET

A diet is a short period of starvation preceding a gain of five pounds.

*   *   *

A diet is what helps a person gain weight more slowly.

*   *   *

You know it is time for a diet when:

- You dive into a swimming pool so your friends can go surfing.
- You have to apply your makeup with a paint roller.
- Weight Watchers demands your resignation.
- You step on a pennyweight scale that gives you your fortune and it says, "One at a time, please!"

- Your face is so full that you look like you're wearing horn-rimmed contact lenses.

- The bus driver asks you to sit on the other side because he wants to make a turn without flipping over.

- You're at school in the classroom and turn around and erase the entire blackboard.

- They throw puffed rice at your wedding.

- You hiccup in your bathing suit, and it looks like someone adjusting a venetian blind.

- You fall down and try to get up, and in the process rock yourself to sleep.

DIETER'S PSALM

My weight is my shepherd;
I shall not want low-calorie foods.
It maketh me to munch on potato chips
   and bean dip;
It leadeth me into 31 Flavors;
It restoreth my soul food;
It leadeth me in the paths of cream
   puffs in bakeries.
Yea, though I waddle through the
   valley of weight watchers,
I will fear no skimmed milk;
For my appetite is with me;
My Hostess "Twinkies" and "Ding
   Dongs," they comfort me;
They anointeth my body with calories;

My scale tippeth over!
Surely chubbiness and contentment
    shall follow me
All the days of my life.
And I shall dwell in the house of
    Marie Callender pies...forever!

DINNER SPEAKER

A dinner speaker was in such a hurry to get to his engagement that when he arrived and sat down at the head table, he suddenly realized that he had forgotten his false teeth.

Turning to the man next to him he said, "I forgot my teeth."

The man said, "No problem." With that he reached into his pocket and pulled out a pair of false teeth. "Try these," he said. The speaker tried them. "Too loose," he said.

The man then said, "I have another pair—try these."

The speaker tried them and responded, "Too tight."

The man was not taken back at all. He then said, "I have one more pair of false teeth—try them."

The speaker said, "They fit perfectly." With that he ate his meal and gave his address.

After the dinner meeting was over, the speaker went over to thank the man who had helped him.

"I want to thank you for coming to my aid. Where is your office? I've been looking for a good dentist."

The man replied, "I'm not a dentist. I'm the local undertaker."

DIPLOMAT

One who never heard that old joke before.

DIRECTIONS

If at first you don't succeed, try looking in the wastebasket for the directions.

DISAGREE

Man to friend: "By the time I found out my father was right, my son was old enough to disagree with me."

* * *

Wife: I'm afraid the mountain air would disagree with me.

Husband: My Dear, it wouldn't dare.

DISBARRED

If lawyers are disbarred and ministers unfrocked, perhaps electricians get delighted ... Far Eastern diplomats disoriented ... cashiers distilled ... alpine climbers dismounted ... piano tuners unstrung ... orchestra leaders disbanded ... artists' models

deposed...cooks deranged...nudists
redressed...office clerks defiled...mediums
dispirited...dressmakers unbiased.

DISCOVERED

A wife is the only person who can look into the
top drawer of a dresser and find a man's socks that
aren't there.

DISPOSITION

They say brunettes have a sweeter disposition
than blondes and redheads. Don't believe it! My
wife has been all three, and I couldn't see any
difference.

DISTINGUISHED

Reporter: And how did you win the
Distinguished Service Cross?
Private: I saved the lives of my entire regiment.
Reporter: Wonderful! And how did you do that?
Private: I shot the cook.

DIVORCE

A couple in Hollywood got divorced, then got
remarried. The divorce didn't work out.

*   *   *

Dopey: Why did the cow get a divorce?
Dopier: She got a bum steer.

*   *   *

What a holler would ensue if people had to pay the minister as much to marry them as they have to pay a lawyer to get them a divorce.

*   *   *

A couple in Hollywood got divorced, then they got remarried. The divorce didn't work out.

DO YOUR BEST

Judge: Thirty years in prison!
Prisoner: But Judge, I won't live that long!
Judge: Don't worry—do what you can.

DOCTOR

People who think that time heals everything haven't tried sitting it out in a doctor's waiting room.

*   *   *

Dr. Hanson: So the operation on the man was just in the nick of time?
Dr. Poure: Yes, in another 24 hours he would have recovered.

DONATION

A millionaire who had been bad all of his life was nearing the end of his time on earth and wanted to wipe the slate clean. To make amends for his evil ways, he donated a lot of money to a local church and had a meeting with the minister to discuss the possibility of getting into heaven.

Since the man had spent most of his life being evil, the minister couldn't really assure him he'd get into heaven, but he didn't want to disappoint the man and lose a big donation. Being diplomatic, the minister sized up the millionaire's chances like this:

"Mr. Jones, when it comes to riding on the heavenly railroad, think of yourself as a standby passenger."

DONKEY

An evangelist was speaking in a meeting when a heckler shouted, "Listen to him! And his father used to drive a wagon led by a donkey."

"That's right," said the evangelist, "and today my father and the wagon are gone. But I see we still have the donkey with us."

DOPEY BLONDE

"What happened to that dopey blonde your husband used to run around with?"

"I dyed my hair!"

DOUBLE TAKE

Life's briefest moment is the time between reading the sign on the freeway and realizing you just missed your exit.

DOUGHNUT

Customer: Waitress, why is my doughnut all smashed?

Waitress: You said you wanted a cup of coffee and a doughnut, and step on it.

DOWN WITH THE SHIP

A soldier who lost his rifle was reprimanded by his captain and told he would have to pay for it.

"Sir," gulped the soldier, "suppose I lost a tank. Surely I would not have to pay for that!"

"Yes, you would, too," bellowed the captain, "even if it took the rest of your life."

"Well," said the soldier, "now I know why the captain goes down with his ship."

DRAGON MILK

Q. How do you get dragon milk?

A. From a cow with short legs!

DRIVING

A man was driving an auto with his wife in the backseat and stalled his car on a railroad track. A train was coming down the track. His wife screamed, "Go on! Go on!"

The husband replied, "You've been driving all day from the backseat. I've got my end across the track. See what you can do with your end."

*   *   *

Driving instructor: What would you do if you were going up an icy hill and the motor stalled and the brakes failed?

Student: I'd quickly adjust the rearview mirror.

DRUMS

Mother: I don't think the man upstairs likes Mike to play on his drums.

Father: Why do you say that?

Mother: Because this afternoon he gave Mike a knife and asked him if he knew what was inside the drum.

DRYER

A sign on a dryer in a coin laundry reads: "This dryer is worthless." A sign on the next dryer reads: "This dryer is next to worthless."

DULL

The trouble with telling a good story is that it reminds the other fellow of a dull one.

*　　*　　*

One girl to another: "There's never a dull moment when you're out with Wilbur...it lasts the whole evening."

DUMB

I didn't say he was dumb. I said he was 20 years old before he could wave good-bye.

DUMB QUESTION

"Did you fall down the elevator shaft?"
"No, I was sitting here and they built it around me."

DUNLAP'S DISEASE

"He is suffering from Dunlap's disease."
"What is Dunlap's disease?"
"His stomach done-laps over his belt!"

DUST

On the way home from church a little boy asked

his mother, "Is it true, Mommy, that we are made of dust?"

"Yes, Darling."

"And do we go back to dust again when we die?"

"Yes, Dear."

"Well, Mommy, when I said my prayers last night and looked under the bed, I found someone who is either coming or going."

DYING

Old Pete was very close to dying but made a miraculous recovery. In the hospital his pastor came to visit him and the conversation went like this:

"Tell me, Pete: When you were so near death's door, did you feel afraid to meet your Maker?"

"No, Pastor," said Pete. "It was the other man I was afraid of!"

DYNAMITE

You know, if brains were dynamite, he wouldn't have enough to blow his nose!

EARACHE

A lady complained of an earache, so the doctor examined her and found a piece of string dangling from her right ear. The doctor began pulling it out, and the more he pulled, the more string came out.

Suddenly the pulling became harder, and he struggled with the string. To his amazement, out fell a bouquet of roses.

The doctor exclaimed, "Good gracious, where did this come from?"

"How should I know?" said the patient. "Why don't you look at the card?"

EARPLUGS

There is a new cigarette with earplugs in every pack. It's for people who don't want to hear why they should quit smoking.

EARTHQUAKE

There was an earthquake recently which frightened inhabitants of a certain town. One couple sent their little boy to stay with an uncle in another district, explaining the reason for the nephew's sudden visit. A day later the parents received this telegram, "Am returning your boy. Send the earthquake."

AN EASIER WAY

Two Smogarians were dragging a deer through the woods by its tail when they ran across another hunter. "It would be easier," said the hunter, "if you would drag the deer by the antlers instead of the tail. Then he won't get caught on all the bushes."

The two Smogarians did as the hunter suggested. After about an hour of dragging the deer by the antlers, one Smogarian said to the other, "This is sure a lot easier."

"Yeah," said the second Smogarian, "but I think we are going the wrong direction."

EATING

Doctors say that if you eat slowly you eat less. You certainly will if you are a member of a large family.

EDUCATION

Adult education is what goes on in a household containing teenage children!

EGGS

Q. Which came first, the chicken or the egg?
A. The chicken, of course. God couldn't lay an egg.

*   *   *

Teacher: Why don't you brush your teeth? I can see what you had for breakfast this morning.
Student: What did I have?
Teacher: Eggs!
Student: You're wrong! That was yesterday!

EGRESS

It is said that Phineas T. Barnum, the famed circus magnate, hung a large sign over one of the exits of his museum which read, "This way to the egress." Many people in the crowds, eager to see what an egress looked like, passed through the door and found themselves out on the street.

ELECTROCUTED

A pastor wired all his pews with electricity. One Sunday from his pulpit he said, "All who will give $100 toward the new building, stand up." He touched a button, and 20 people sprang up.

"Fine, fine," the preacher beamed. "Now all who will give $500, stand up." He touched another button and 20 more jumped to their feet.

"Excellent," he shouted. "Now all who will give $1,000, stand up." He threw the master switch and electrocuted 15 deacons.

*   *   *

Q. Why do elephants have flat feet?
A. From jumping out of trees.

*   *   *

Q. Why is it dangerous to go into the jungle between two and four in the afternoon?

A. Because that's when elephants are jumping out of trees.

*　　*　　*

Q. Why are pygmies so small?

A. They went into the jungle between two and four in the afternoon.

ELEPHANT EARS

Customer: Your sign says, "$50 to anyone who orders something we can't furnish." I would like to have an elephant ear sandwich.

Waiter: Ohhh...we're going to have to pay you the $50.

Customer: No elephant ears, huh?

Waiter: Oh, we've got lots of them...but we're all out of those big buns!

ELEPHANTS

Customer: Your sign says you will cook any type of steak? I'll try an elephant steak.

Waiter: Will that be African or Indian?

EMBARRASSING

Nothing is as embarrassing as watching your boss do something you assured him couldn't be done.

EMPIRE STATE BUILDING

Did you hear about the man who jumped from the Empire State Building and lived to tell about it? He told the people on the ninety-third floor, those on the eighty-fourth floor, everyone on the sixty-second floor, and those on...

EMPTY SPACE

"I have a cold or something in my head."
"I bet it's a cold."

ENDS

Why is it that every time you start to make ends meet, somebody comes along and moves the ends?

ENDURE

First member: I thought the sermon was divine. It reminded me of the peace of God. It passed all understanding.

Second member: It reminded me of the mercies of God. I thought it would endure forever.

ENEMIES

The Bible tells us to love our neighbors and also to love our enemies, probably because they are generally the same people.

ENGAGEMENT RING

A big-game hunter recently returned from Africa and went to a psychiatrist. He told the psychiatrist he didn't want to go through analysis, but would pay him $200 for answering two questions.

The psychiatrist said this was highly irregular, but he agreed to do it.

"Is it possible," the hunter asked, "for a man to be in love with an elephant?"

The psychiatrist said, "Absolutely impossible. In all the annals of medicine, I've never heard of it. The whole idea is ridiculous. What's your second question?"

The man then asked meekly, "Do you know anyone who wants to buy a very large engagement ring?"

*   *   *

Mary: Well, what happened when you showed the girls in the office your new engagement ring? Did they all admire it?

Sara: Better than that, four of them recognized it.

ENJOYABLE

For a minute I didn't recognize you. It was my most enjoyable minute today.

ENOUGH SAID

A certain man had a great reputation for always catching his limit of fish. Everyone wanted to know his secret. One day the game warden asked to go along to see where he was fishing.

The man and the game warden got into a boat and rowed to the middle of a nearby lake. The fisherman threw over an anchor, and then reached into a paper sack. He pulled out a stick of dynamite, lit a match to the fuse, and tossed it into the lake. There was a huge explosion and several fish floated to the surface.

The game warden was irate. He yelled, "You can't do that! It's against the law!"

The fisherman than reached into the sack and pulled out another stick of dynamite. He lit the fuse and then threw it into the lap of the game warden. As he did this he asked, "Are you going to talk or fish?"

ENTRANCE TO SALE

Business was pretty bad at Max's Bargain Emporium. Then, to compound his troubles, Harry's on his right decided to run a big Going-Out-Of-Business Sale and hung up a sign reading: THE GREATEST GOING-OUT-OF-BUSINESS SALE EVER. YOU COULDN'T GET BIGGER BARGAINS IF WE WERE REALLY GOING OUT OF BUSINESS.

Then Leo, on Max's left, decided to run a sale and hung up a sign reading: FIRE SALE. YOU COULDN'T GET BETTER BUYS EVEN IF THERE WAS A REAL FIRE.

Max joined the fun. He hung up a sign directly between the others reading: ENTRANCE TO SALE.

ESCAPE

The news media featured a convict's daring daylight escape from prison and his voluntary return and surrender later that evening. When reporters asked him why he had come back, he said, "The minute I sneaked home to see my wife, the first thing she said was, 'Where have you been? You escaped eight hours ago!' "

EXASPERATING

Nothing is more exasperating than getting in the lane behind a guy who is observing the speed limit.

EXCELLENT TIME

The loudspeaker of the big jet clicked on and the captain's voice announced in a clear, even tone: "Now there's no cause for alarm, but we felt you passengers should know that for the last three hours we've been flying without the benefit of radio, compass, radar, or navigational beam due to the breakdown of certain key components. This means that we are, in the broad sense of the word, lost and are not quite sure in which direction we are heading. I'm sure you'll be glad to know, however...on the brighter side of the picture...that we're making excellent time!"

EXCUSE ME

A meek little man in a restaurant timidly touched the arm of a man puting on an overcoat. "Excuse me," he said, "but do you happen to be Mr. Smith of Newport?"

"No, I'm not!" the man answered impatiently.

"Oh-er-well," stammered the first man, "you see, I am, and that's his overcoat you're putting on."

EXECUTIVE

An executive is a person who can take two hours for lunch without anybody missing him.

EXPERIENCE

Experience is the thing you have left when everything else is gone.

*   *   *

A young man came to interview a bank president.

"Tell me, Sir, how did you become so successful?"

"Two words."

"And what are they, Sir?"

"Right decisions."

"How do you make right decisions?"

"One word... experience."

"And how do you get experience?"

"Two words."

"And what are they?"

"Wrong decisions!"

EXPORT

The principal export of the United States is money.

EXTREME PENALTY

The extreme penalty for bigamy is two mothers-in-law.

EYE SORE

"Every time I have a cup of coffee, I get a stabbing pain in my right eye. What shall I do?"

"Take the spoon out of your cup."

FACE

If your face is your fortune, you won't have to pay any income tax.

*　　*　　*

"Your face would stop a clock."
"And yours would make one run!"

*   *   *

Is that your face, or did your neck throw up?

*   *   *

The popular preacher, Charles Spurgeon, was admonishing a class of divinity students on the importance of making their facial expressions harmonize with their speech in delivering sermons. "When you speak of heaven," he said, "let your face light up and be irradiated with a heavenly gleam. Let your eyes shine with reflected glory. And when you speak of hell...well, then your everyday face will do."

FACE-LIFT

"My uncle had his face lifted."
"How did they do it?"
"With a piece of rope around his neck."

FALSE

Q. What do we call the last teeth to appear in the mouth?
A. False.

FALSE TEETH

At a Sunday school picnic the minister, while walking across a small footbridge, was seized with a fit of sneezing. His false teeth flew from his mouth and landed in the clear water in the middle of the stream. Much worried and embarrassed, the minister was preparing to remove his shoes and wade in after his dentures when a dear little gray-haired grandmother appeared on the scene, carrying a well-filled dinner basket. When she discovered the minister's plight, she reached in her basket, removed a crisp, brown chicken leg, tied a string to it and tossed it into the water near the dentures. Quickly the teeth clamped into the chicken leg and were hauled to safety.

FAMILIAR

I don't recall your face, but your breath is familiar!

FAMILY TREE

The cheapest way to have your family tree traced is to run for a public office.

FAMOUS LAST WORDS

"You can make it easy—that train isn't coming fast."

"Gimmee a match. I think my gas tank is empty."

"Wife, these biscuits are tough."

"Let's see if it's loaded."

"Step on her, boy, we're only going 75."

"Just watch me dive from that bridge."

"If you knew anything, you wouldn't be a traffic cop."

"Lemme have that bottle; I'll try it."

"What? Your mother is going to stay another month?"

"Say, who's boss of this joint, anyhow?"

FANS

What makes a baseball stadium cool?

Answer: The fans.

FAULTS

"Once a friend of mine and I agreed it would be helpful for each of us to tell the other all our faults."

"How did it work?"

"We haven't spoken for five years."

A FEW POUNDS

Wife: Honey, will you still love me after I put on a few pounds?

Husband: Yes, I do.

FIDDLE AROUND

When Joe was a little boy, he took fiddle lessons. One day while he was practicing, scraping dismally back and forth with his bow, his dog set up a plaintive wailing and howling. Finally Joan, who was trying to do her homework, stuck her head into the room where her brother was practicing.

"For goodness' sake!" she complained. "Can't you play something the dog doesn't know?"

FINE

A fine is a tax for doing wrong. A tax is a fine for doing well.

*   *   *

I'm fine, I'm fine.
There's nothing whatever the matter with me.
I'm just as healthy as I can be.
I have arthritis in both of my knees,
And when I talk, I talk with a wheeze.
My pulse is weak and my blood is thin,
But I'm awfully well for the shape I'm in.
My teeth eventually will have to come out,
And I can't hear a word unless you shout.
I'm overweight and I can't get thin,
But I'm awfully well for the shape I'm in.
Arch supports I have for both my feet
Or I wouldn't be able to walk down the street.

Sleep is denied me every night,
And every morning I'm really a sight.
My memory is bad and my head's a-spin,
And I practically live on aspirin,
But I'm awfully well for the shape I'm in.
The moral is, as this tale unfolds,
That for you and me who are growing old,
It's better to say "I'm fine" with a grin
Than to let people know the shape we're in!

FINISHED

A man is incomplete until he's married...then he's finished.

* * *

A little boy in church, awaking after a nap, asked his father, "Has the preacher finished?"
"Yes, Son, he has finished, but he hasn't stopped."

FIRE INSURANCE

Bob: Does your uncle carry life insurance?
Paul: No, he just carries fire insurance. He knows where he is going.

FIRST BABY

The phone rang in the maternity ward and an

excited voice on the other end said: "This is George Smith and I'm bringing my wife in...she's about to have a baby!"

"Calm down," replied the attendant. "Tell me, is this her first baby?"

"No," the voice replied, "this is her husband."

FISH

Once upon a time there was a fisherman who had two sons named Toward and Away. Every day he would go fishing and return late at night, always talking about the giant fish he had almost caught. One day he took Toward and Away fishing with him.

That night he returned home more excited than ever.

"Sally," he yelled to his wife, "you should have seen the fish I saw today. A tremendous gray fish, ten feet long with horns and fur all over its back. It had legs like a caterpillar. It came crawling out of the water, snatched our son Toward, and swallowed him in one gulp!"

"Good gracious!" exclaimed his wife. "That's horrible!"

"Oh, that was nothing," said her husband. "You should have seen the one that got Away!"

FISHING

Two men fishing on Sunday morning were

feeling pretty guilty, especially since the fish didn't bite. One said to the other, "I guess I should have stayed home and gone to church."

To which the other angler replied lazily, "I couldn't have gone to church anyway. My wife's sick in bed."

FIVE HUNDRED TIMES

In the traffic court of a large Midwestern city, a young lady was brought before the judge because of a ticket given her for driving through a red light. She explained to His Honor that she was a schoolteacher and requested an immediate disposal of her case in order that she might hasten on to her classes. A wild gleam came into the judge's eye. "You're a schoolteacher, eh?" said he. "Madam, I shall realize my lifelong ambition. I've waited years to have a schoolteacher in this court. Sit down at that table and write 'I went through a red light' 500 times!"

FLAGSTONE

A husband put in a flagstone walk from house to street. When he finished, he called his wife to come look. "It is terrible, the colors don't match, and the stones are crooked."

Weary and disappointed he asked, "How is it for length?"

FLASHLIGHT

A boy from New York was being led through the swamps of Georgia.

"Is it true," he asked, "that an alligator won't attack you if you carry a flashlight?"

"That depends," replied the guide, "on how fast you carry the flashlight."

FLIRT

Sally: I wonder what's wrong with that tall blond guy over there. Just a minute ago he was getting awful friendly, and then all of a sudden he turned pale, walked away, and won't even look at me anymore.

Linda: Maybe he saw me come in. He's my husband.

FLIRTING

The minister arose to address his congregation. "There is a certain man among us today who is flirting with another man's wife. Unless he puts five dollars in the collection box, his name will be read from the pulpit."

When the collection plate came in, there were 19 five-dollar bills, and a two-dollar bill with this note attached: "Other three on payday."

FOILED AGAIN

Q. What did the man say when he lost the fencing match?

A. Foiled again.

FOOL

Reverend Henry Ward Beecher entered Plymouth Church one Sunday and found several letters awaiting him. He opened one and found it contained the single word "Fool." Quietly and with becoming seriousness, he announced to the congregation that fact in these words:

"I have known many an instance of a man writing a letter and forgetting to sign his name, but this is the only instance I have ever known of a man signing his name and forgetting to write the letter."

* * *

Women are fools to marry men. On the other hand, what else is there to marry?

FOOTBALL

The pastor of the Calvary Baptist Church in Tulsa calls this his "football theology":

Draft choice: Selection of a pew near to (or away from) air-conditioning vents.

Bench-warmer: Inactive member.

In the pocket: Where too many Christians keep their tithes.

Fumble: Lousy sermon.

Two-minute warning: Deacon in front row taking a peek at his watch in full view of the preacher.

FORGETFUL

"George is so forgetful," the sales manager complained to his secretary. "It's a wonder he can sell anything. I asked him to pick me up some sandwiches on his way back from lunch, and I'm not sure he'll even remember to come back."

Just then the door flew open, and in bounced George. "You'll never guess what happened!" he shouted. "While I was at lunch, I met Old Man Brown, who hasn't bought anything from us for five years. Well, we got to talking and he gave me this half-million-dollar order!"

"See," sighed the sales manager to his secretary. "I told you he'd forget the sandwiches."

*   *   *

At a commuter train station a policeman noticed a woman driver bowed over the steering wheel of her car.

"Is there anything wrong?" said the policeman.

Half crying and half laughing the woman responded, "For ten years I have driven my husband to the station to catch his train. This morning I forgot him!"

FORK

If you drop a fork, it's a sign company is coming. If a fork is missing, it's a sign company is going.

FORTUNE

Wife to husband who just got off the pennyweight scale: "Your fortune says that you are handsome, debonair, and wealthy. It even has your weight wrong!"

FOUR TO GO

Sue: See that woman over there? She's been married four times—once to a millionaire, then to an actor, then to a minister, and last to an undertaker.

Sal: I know! One for the money, two for the show, three to get ready, and four to go!

FOUR TYPES OF MINISTERS

Ministers fall into four categories:

1. Those who do not have any notes and the people have no idea how long they will speak.

2. Those who put down on the podium in front of them each page of their sermon as they read it. These honest ones enable the audience to keep track of how much more is to come.

3. Those who cheat by putting each sheet of notes under the others in their hand.

4. And, worst of all, those who put down each sheet of notes as they read it and then horrify the audience by picking up the whole batch and reading off the other side.

FOURTEEN FEET

"Will you tell the court how far you were taken from the spot where the shooting occurred?" asked the defense counsel.

"I was exactly fourteen feet, three-and-one-half inches," replied the witness.

"How can you be sure of the exact distance?" asked the lawyer.

"I measured it because I was sure sooner or later some fool would ask that question."

FRUGAL

The man walked into the house panting and almost completely exhausted. "What happened, Honey?" inquired his wife.

"It's a great new idea I have," he gasped. "I ran all the way home behind the bus and saved 50 cents."

"That wasn't very bright," replied his wife. "Why didn't you run behind a taxi and save three dollars?"

*   *   *

A rather frugal man asked the bank for a loan of one dollar and was told he would have to pay seven percent interest at the end of the year. For security he offered $60,000 in U.S. bonds. The banker, foreseeing a potential depositor, accepted the bonds and gave the man a dollar.

At the end of the year, he was back with a dollar and seven cents to clear up his debt and asked for the return of his bonds. Upon returning the bonds the banker asked, "I don't want to be inquisitive, but since you have all those bonds, why did you have to borrow a dollar?"

"Well," said the tightfisted old gent, "I really didn't have to. But do you know of any other way I could get the use of a safety deposit box for seven cents a year?"

FUNERAL

"Do you believe in life after death?" the boss asked one of his younger employees.

"Yes, Sir."

"Well, then, that makes everything just fine," the boss went on. "About an hour after you left yesterday to go to your grandfather's funeral, he stopped in to see you."

*   *   *

A young minister, in the first days of his first parish, was obliged to call upon the widow of an eccentric man who had just died. Standing before the open casket and consoling the widow, he said, "I know this must be a very hard blow, Mrs. Vernon. But we must remember that what we see here is the husk only, the shell—the nut has gone to heaven."

GALAXIES

NASA reports that galaxies are speeding away from earth at 90,000 miles a second. What do you suppose they know that we don't?

GARAGE SALE

A garage sale is a technique for distributing all the junk in your garage among all the other garages in the neighborhood.

GARBAGE COLLECTION

If the garbage workers in your community ever go on strike, you might like to know how a wise New Yorker disposed of his refuse for the nine days the sanitation workers were off the job last summer.

Each day he wrapped his garbage in gift paper, then he put it in a shopping bag. When he parked his car, he left the bag on the front seat with the window open. When he got back to the car, the garbage always had been collected.

GAS

Right in the middle of the service and just before the sermon, a member of the congregation remembered she had forgotten to turn off the gas under the roast. Hurriedly she scribbled a note and passed it to the usher to give to her husband. Unfortunately, the usher misunderstood her intention and took it to the pulpit. Unfolding the note, the preacher read aloud, "Please go home and turn off the gas."

GAS PRICES

Gas prices are so high that when I pulled into a station this morning and asked for a dollar's worth, the attendant dabbed some behind my ears.

GENERATION

The older generation thought nothing of getting up at five every morning—and the younger generation doesn't think much of it either.

*   *   *

Our generation never got a break. When we were young they taught us to respect our elders. Now that we're older, they tell us to listen to the youth of the country.

GEORGE

A man in a supermarket was pushing a cart which contained, among other things, a screaming baby. As the man proceeded along the aisles, he kept repeating softly, "Keep calm, George. Don't get excited, George. Don't yell, George."

A lady watched with admiration and then said, "You are certainly to be commended for your patience in trying to quiet little George."

"Lady," he declared, "*I'm* George!"

GERMS

Husband: Don't put that money in your mouth. There are germs on it.

Wife: Don't be silly. Even a germ can't live on the money you earn.

GETTING EVEN

Judge: Haven't I seen you before?

Man: Yes, Your Honor. I taught your daughter how to play the piano.

Judge: Thirty years.

GHOST

A photographer went to a haunted castle

determined to get a picture of a ghost which was said to appear only once in a hundred years. Not wanting to frighten off the spook, the photographer sat in the dark until midnight when the apparition became visible.

The ghost turned out to be friendly and consented to pose for a snapshot. The happy photographer popped a bulb into his camera and took the picture. Then he dashed to his studio, developed the negative...and groaned. It was underexposed and completely blank.

Moral: The spirit was willing but the flash was weak.

*   *   *

The patient explained to the psychiatrist that he was haunted by visions of his departed relatives.

Patient: These ghosts are perched on the tops of fence posts around my garden every night. They just sit there and watch me and watch me and watch me. What can I do?

Psychiatrist: That's easy—just sharpen the tops of the posts.

GLASS EYE

Christy: That lady has a glass eye.

Lisa: How did you find that out?

Christy: Well, it just came out in the conversation.

GNU

Mama Gnu was waiting for Papa Gnu as he came home for dinner one evening.

"Our little boy was very bad today," she declared. "I want you to punish him."

"Oh no," said Papa Gnu. "I won't punish him. You'll have to learn to paddle your own gnu."

GOLD

A member of the Inca tribe was captured by the Spanish. The captain told his interpreter to say to the Inca Indian, "Tell him if he doesn't tell us where they have hidden all of their gold, that we will burn both of his feet in the fire."

Through the interpreter the Inca Indian responded, "I'd rather die than tell you where the gold is." With that, they burned his feet in the fire.

The captain then told the interpreter to say, "Tell him that if he doesn't tell us where the gold is hidden, that we will hang him from that noose on the tree over there."

The Inca Indian again responded, "I'd rather die than tell you where the gold is." With that, they took him over to the tree and hung him until he could hardly breathe.

The Spanish captain then ordered the Indian to be brought to him again. This time he said to the interpreter, "Tell him if he doesn't tell us where the gold is that we will skin him alive."

The Inca Indian could stand it no longer and said, "The gold is hidden in a little cave just behind the large waterfall. The waterfall is one mile over the hill to the right."

The interpreter related the following to the captain: "He said that he would rather die than tell you where the gold is."

GOLF

Golf is a lot of walking, broken up by disappointment and bad arithmetic.

*   *   *

Man to friend: "After three sets of clubs and ten years of lessons, I'm finally getting some fun out of golf. I quit."

*   *   *

Friend: Pastor, how do you let off steam when you miss a shot and your golf ball goes into a sand trap?

Pastor: I just repeat the names of some of the members of my congregation...with feeling!

*   *   *

A group of golfers were telling tall stories. At last came a veteran's turn. "Well," he said, "I once drove a ball, accidentally of course, through a cottage window. The ball knocked over an oil lamp and the place caught on fire."

"What did you do?" asked his friends.

"Oh," said the veteran, "I immediately teed another ball, took careful aim, and hit the fire alarm on Main Street. That brought out the fire engine before any major damage was done."

*   *   *

Wife: George, you promised you'd be home at 4:00. It's now 8:00.

George: Honey, please listen to me. Poor ol' Fred is dead. He just dropped over on the eighth green.

Wife: Oh, that's awful.

George: It surely was. For the rest of the game it was hit the ball, drag Fred, hit the ball, drag Fred.

*   *   *

A distinguished clergyman and one of his parishioners were playing golf. It was a very close match, and at the last hole the clergyman teed up, addressed the ball, and swung his driver with great force. The ball, instead of sailing down the fairway, merely rolled off the tee and settled slowly some 12 feet away.

The clergyman frowned, glared, and bit his lip, but said nothing. His opponent regarded him for a moment, and then remarked:

"Pastor, that is the most profane silence I have ever witnessed."

GOOD

The man who says he is just as good as half the folks in the church seldom specifies which half.

A GOOD DAY

The man of the house finally took all his family's disabled umbrellas to the repair shop. Two days later, on the way to his office, when he got up to leave the streetcar, he absentmindedly laid hold of the umbrella belonging to a woman beside him. The women cried "Stop, thief!" and rescued her umbrella, which covered the man with shame and confusion.

The same day, he stopped at the repair shop and received all eight of his umbrellas duly repaired. As he entered a streetcar with the unwrapped umbrellas tucked under his arm, he was horrified to behold the lady of his morning adventure glaring at him. Her voice came to him charged with withering scorn: "Huh! Had a good day, didn't you!"

GOOD DEAL

A man I know solved the problem of too many visiting relatives. He borrowed money from the rich ones and loaned it to the poor ones. Now none of them come back.

GOOD HEAVENS

After a long evening of conversation the host said, "I hate to put you out, but I have to get up at six o'clock in the morning to catch a plane."

"Good heavens," said the guest. "I thought you were at *my* house!"

GOOD JOKE

After the dinner is over,
After the waiters have gone,
After the coffee and mint-drops,
After the very last song;
Then come the speeches and laughter,
And we settle ourselves for a Coke,
In the hope that one of the speakers
Will tell us a really good joke.

A GOOD LAUGH

"My husband just ran off with someone else. I can hardly control myself."

"Go ahead and let go, Dearie. You'll feel better after a good laugh."

*   *   *

"What would you say if I asked you to be my wife?"

"Nothing. I can't talk and laugh at the same time."

A GOOD LESSON

Girl: Did you kiss me when the lights were out?
Boy: No!
Girl: It must have been that fellow over there!
Boy (starting to get up): I'll teach him a thing or two!
Girl: You couldn't teach him a thing!

GOOD NEWS

Bad news: Your wife just ran off with your best friend.

Good news: That's two people off your Christmas list.

GOOD OLD DAYS

Too many people keep looking back to the good old days:

1880…"I walked 14 miles through snow and rain to go to school."

1915…"I had to walk five miles every day."

1936…"It was 11 blocks to the bus stop every morning."

1950…"I had to buy gasoline for my own car."

1966…"When I drove to school as a boy, we didn't have power brakes, power steering, or power windows."

GOOD SPORT

The trouble with being a good sport is that you have to lose to prove it.

GOOD THINKING

"Your age, please?" asked the census taker.

"Well," said the woman, "let me figure it out. I was 18 when I was married and my husband was 30. He is now 60, or twice as old as he was then, so I am now 36."

*   *   *

Panting and perspiring, two men on a tandem bicycle at last got to the top of a steep hill.

"That was a stiff climb," said the first man.

"It certainly was," replied the second man. "And if I hadn't kept the brake on, we would have slid down backward."

GORILLAS

A gorilla walked into a drugstore and ordered a 50-cent sundae. He put down a ten-dollar bill to pay for it. The clerk thought, "What can a gorilla know about money?" So he handed back a single dollar in change.

As he did, he said, "You know, we don't get many gorillas in here."

"No wonder," answered the gorilla, "at nine dollars a sundae."

GOSSIP

"I think we need to change the morning hymn," said the minister to his song leader. "My topic this morning is 'gossip.' I don't think 'I Love to Tell the Story' would be the best song."

*   *   *

First man: I think we should all confess our faults one to another. I've got a terrible habit of stealing!

Second man: I've got a terrible habit of lying!

Third man: I beat my wife!

Fourth man: When no one is around, I get drunk!

Fifth Man: I've got the terrible habit of gossiping, and I can hardly wait to get out of here!

GOTCHA

Two married girls were bothering a third girl who was still a spinster.

"Now, tell us truthfully," they badgered her, "have you ever really had a chance to marry?"

With a withering glance, she retorted, "Suppose you ask your husbands."

GOVERNMENT

It's becoming more and more difficult to support the government in the style to which it has become accustomed.

GRASS HOUSES

Did you hear about the tribe in Africa that stole the king's throne from a rival tribe? They hid the throne in the rafters of their grass hut. The men who stole the throne were having a party in the hut. They were feeling happy about their successful theft when all of a sudden the rafters broke and the throne fell down and killed all of the men.

Moral: Those who live in grass houses shouldn't stow thrones.

GRATEFUL

Pity the poor atheist who feels grateful but has no one to thank.

GRAY HAIR

"I wonder if my husband will love me when my hair is gray."

"Why not? He's loved you through three shades already."

GROCERY MONEY

Husband: What have you been doing with all the grocery money I gave you?

Wife: Turn sideways and look in the mirror.

GROWING OLDER

An elderly gentleman wasn't feeling well, and became irritated with his doctor because he wasn't getting better after five visits.

"Look!" said the doctor. "I'm doing all I can to help you. I can't make you younger."

"I wasn't particularly interested in getting younger," said the old man. "I just want to continue growing older."

GROWN-UP

"My son is really growing up. Only last week he was able to go to the psychiatrist all by himself."

GRUMPY

Marriage counselor to female client: Maybe your problem is that you've been waking up grumpy in the morning.

Client: "No, I always let him sleep."

GUARDIAN ANGEL

Wife: Aren't you driving a little too fast, Dear?

Husband: Don't you believe in a guardian angel? He'll take care of us.

Wife: Yes, I do. But I'm afraid we left him miles back!

GUNNYSACK

I learned how to swim the old way when I was about five years old. My Dad took me out to the middle of a lake in a boat and then threw me in the water. The swim back to shore was not too bad—it was getting out of the gunnysack.

GURU

Guru to guest: "There are several meanings of life—a 50-dollar meaning, a 100-dollar meaning, and a very meaningful 500-dollar meaning."

HAIRCUT

Did you hear about the rock 'n' roll singer who wore a hearing aid for three years? Then he found out he only needed a haircut.

HAIRDO

We're constantly amazed at these young things with their fancy hairdos and skin-tight pants—and the girls are even worse.

HALF-WIT

Why don't you pal around with a half-wit so you can have someone to look up to!

*   *   *

He spends half his time trying to be witty. You might say he's a half-wit.

A HAMMER FROM SEARS

A man was sitting in a café when all of a sudden someone came in and beat him up. When he woke up, he said to the owner, "Who was that?"

"That was Kung Fu from China," replied the owner.

Next week the man was eating in the same café when a different person entered and beat him up. When he woke up, he said to the owner, "Who was that?"

The owner said, "That was Kuang Chow from Taiwan."

Several weeks later Kung Fu and Kuang Chow were eating in the café. The man who had been beaten by both of them entered and paid them back the abuse. He said to the owner, "When they wake up, tell them that that was 'a hammer from Sears.'"

HANGED

The applicant for life insurance was finding it difficult to fill out the application. The salesman asked what the trouble was, and the man said that he couldn't answer the question about the cause of death of his father.

The salesman wanted to know why. After some embarrassment the client explained that his father had been hanged.

The salesman pondered for a moment. "Just write: 'Father was taking part in a public function when the platform gave way.' "

HANS SCHMIDT

A man was walking down the street and noticed a sign reading: "Hans Schmidt's Chinese Laundry." Being of a curious nature, he entered and was greeted by an obviously Oriental man who identified himself as Hans Schmidt.

"How come you have a name like that?" inquired the stranger.

The Oriental explained in very broken English that when he landed in America he was standing in the immigration line behind a German. When asked his name, the German replied, "Hans Schmidt." When the immigration official asked the Oriental his name, he replied, "Sam Ting."

HAPPY

"Now, that looks like a happily married couple."
"Don't be too sure, My Dear. They're probably saying the same thing about us."

HARSH

Husband: Now look, Lucy. I don't want to seem harsh, but your mother has been living with us for 20 years now. Don't you think it's about time she got a place of her own?

Wife: *My* mother? I thought she was *your* mother!

HATBAND

Did you hear about the man who complained that every time he put on his hat he heard music? The doctor fixed him up: He removed his hatband.

HATCHET

There's no point in burying a hatchet if you're going to put up a marker on the site.

HAY

One Sunday as a farmer was getting in his hay crop, his minister stopped by. The pastor asked the farmer if he had been to church. "To tell the truth,

I would rather sit on the hay load and think about the church than sit in the church and think about hay."

HEAVEN

A new group of male applicants had just arrived in heaven.

Peter looked them over and ordered, "All men who were henpecked on earth, please step to the left; all those who were bosses in their own homes, step to the right."

The line quickly formed on the left. Only one man stepped to the right.

Peter looked at the frail little man standing by himself and inquired, "What makes you think you belong on that side?"

Without hesitation, the meek little man explained, "Because this is where my wife told me to stand."

HEIR

Stranger: Good morning, Doctor. I just dropped in to tell you how much I benefited from your treatment.

Doctor: But you're not one of my patients.

Stranger: I know. But my Uncle Bill was, and I'm his heir.

HELL

A very foul-mouthed man met the local pastor

on the street one day and said, "Now, where in hell have I seen you?" To which the pastor replied, "From where in hell do you come, Sir?"

HELP WITH THE DISHES

Wife: Would you help me with the dishes?
Husband: That isn't a man's job.
Wife: The Bible suggests that it is.
Husband: Where does it say that?
Wife: In 2 Kings 21:13 it says, "And I will wipe Jerusalem as a man wipeth a dish, wiping it and turning it upside down."

HER LAST DAY

"Why are you so sad, Bill?"
"My wife said she wouldn't talk to me for 30 days."
"Why should that make you sad?"
"Today is her last day!"

HICCUPS

A man rushed into a drugstore and asked a pharmacist for something to stop hiccups. The druggist poured a glass of water and threw it into the man's face.

"Why did you do that?" the man exploded angrily.

"Well, you don't have hiccups now, do you?"

"No!" shouted the customer. "But my wife out in the car still does!"

HIPPOPOTAMUS

There were three Indian squaws: one sitting on an elk hide, one on a deer hide, and one on a hippopotamus hide. The two squaws on the elk and deer hides had one papoose each, while the squaw on the hippopotamus hide had two papooses.

Moral: The squaw on the hippopotamus equals the sum of the squaws on the other two hides.

HITLER

Adolph Hitler was an avid believer in astrology and consulted with his special astrologist before making any decisions. One day in consulting with him, Hitler asked, "On what day will I die?"

"You will die on a Jewish holiday," replied the astrologist.

"How can you be so sure of that?" asked Hitler.

"Any day you die will be a Jewish holiday," replied the astrologist.

HO! HO! HO!

A man returned to his sports car to find a freshly crushed fender and this note affixed to his windshield wiper: "The people who saw me sideswipe your fender are now watching me write

this note, and doubtless figure I'm telling you
my name and address so you can contact me and
send me the bill. Ho! Ho! Ho! You should live so
long."

HOG CALLER

A local pastor joined a community service club,
and the members thought they would have some
fun with him. Under his name on the badge they
printed "Hog Caller" as his occupation.

Everyone made a big fanfare as the badge was
presented. The pastor responded by saying: "I
usually am called the 'Shepherd of the Sheep'...but
you know your people better than I do."

HONORARY DEGREE

An honorary degree is like the curl in the tail of
a pig:

> It follows the main part of the animal;
> It is highly ornamental;
> In no way does it improve the quality of
> the ham.

HORSE SENSE

Q. What is another name for stable thinking?
A. Horse sense.

HORSERADISH

Marriage is like horseradish: Men praise it with tears in their eyes.

*   *   *

A minister who was very fond of pure, hot horseradish always kept a bottle of it on his dining room table. He offered some to a guest, who took a big spoonful.

When the guest finally was able to speak, he gasped, "I've heard many ministers preach hellfire, but you are the first one I've met who passed out a sample of it."

HOURS

Applicant: Before I take this job, tell me: Are the hours long?

Employer: No, only 60 minutes each.

HOUSE CALLS

Nothing annoys a woman more than to have friends drop in unexpectedly and find the house looking as it usually does.

HOUSEWIFE

The United States is the only country where a

housewife hires a woman to do her cleaning so she can do volunteer work at the day nursery where the cleaning woman leaves her child.

HOW ABOUT A DATE?

A cute girl was giving a manicure to a man in the barbershop.

The man said, "How about a date later?"

She said, "I'm married."

"So call up your husband and tell him you're going to visit a girlfriend."

She said, "You tell him yourself. He's shaving you."

HUDSON RIVER

A boastful Britisher was holding forth on the merits of his watch to friends in New York City. At last one of the Americans decided he could stand it no longer.

"That's nothing," he interrupted. "I dropped my watch into the Hudson a year ago, and it's been running ever since."

The Englishman looked taken aback.

"What?" he exclaimed. "The same watch?"

"No," he replied, "the Hudson."

HUGGING

Buck: Did you ever wonder why there are so many more auto wrecks than railway accidents?

Bill: Did you ever hear of the fireman hugging the engineer?

HUNGRY

First man: I'm so hungry I could eat a horse.
Second man: I'm so hungry I could eat a moose.
Third man: I'm so hungry I could eat a bear.
Woman: I've just lost my appetite.

HUNTER

First hunter: How do you know you hit that duck?
Second hunter: Because I shot him in the foot and in the head at the same time.
First hunter: How could you possibly hit him in the foot and head at the same time?
Second hunter: He was scratching his head.

HYMN

Three churches, all different denominations, were located on the same main intersection. One Sunday morning a passerby heard the first church singing, "Will There Be Any Stars in My Crown?"

The next church was singing, "No, Not One."

From the third church came, "Oh, That Will Be Glory for Me."

* * *

A song leader had a very rough time once when he was leading a choir and didn't pay attention to the words of the song. He said, "I want the women to sing the verse 'I will go home today,' and the men to come in on the chorus with 'Glad day, Glad day.'" The people were laughing too much to sing the song.

I DON'T GET IT

Wife to husband: "Look, Ralph, the first garden tools are peeping their heads above the snow."

I GET IT

Q. How do you make an Englishman happy in his old age?

A. Tell him jokes when he is still young.

I MEAN

It is not always easy to say the right thing on the spur of the moment. We can sympathize with the chap who met an old friend after many years.

"How is your wife?"

"She is in heaven," replied the friend.

"Oh, I'm sorry," stammered the chap. Then he realized this was not the thing to say. "I mean," he stammered, "I'm glad." That seemed even worse so he blurted, "Well, what I really mean is, 'I'm surprised.'"

I WOULD LIKE TO NOT RAISE HOGS!

(Letter sent to the Secretary of Agriculture)

Dear Mr. Secretary:

My friend Bordereaux received a $1,000 check from the government for not raising hogs, and so I am going into the not-raising-hogs business.

What I want to know is, what is the best kind of land not to raise hogs on and what is the best kind of hogs not to raise? I would prefer not to raise razorback, but if this is not the best kind not to raise, I will just as gladly not raise Durocs or Poland Chinas.

The hardest part of this business is going to be keeping an individual record on each of the hogs I do not raise.

My friend Bordereaux has been raising hogs for more than 20 years and the most he ever made was $400 in 1918, until this year when he received $1,000 for not raising hogs. Now, if I get $1,000 for not raising 50 hogs, I will get $2,000 for not raising 100 hogs, etc.

I plan to start off on a small scale, holding myself down to not raising 4,000 hogs for which I will, of course, receive $80,000.

Now these hogs I will not raise will not eat 100,000 bushels of corn. I understand you pay farmers for not raising corn. Will you pay me for not raising 100,000 bushels of corn, which I will not feed to the hogs which I am not raising?

I want to get started as soon as possible, as this looks like a good time of year for not raising hogs.

Yours very truly,
Octover Brussard

I'M FOR IT

A parishioner had dozed off to sleep during the morning service.

"Will all who want to go to heaven stand?" the preacher asked.

All stood, except the sleeping parishioner.

After they sat down, the pastor continued: "Well, will all who want to go to the other place stand?"

Somebody suddenly dropped a songbook, and the sleeping man jumped to his feet and stood sheepishly facing the preacher. He mumbled confusedly, "Well, Preacher, I don't know what we're voting for, but it looks like you and I are the only ones for it."

I'M IMPRESSED

A blowhard Air Force major was promoted to colonel and received a brand-new office. His first morning behind the desk, an airman knocked on the door and asked to speak to him. The colonel, feeling the urge to impress the young airman, picked up his phone and said:

"Yes, General, thank you. Yes I will pass that along to the President this afternoon. Yes, good-bye, Sir."

Then turning to the airman, he barked, "And what do you want?"

"Nothing important, Sir," said the airman. "I just came to install your telephone."

I'M NOT STUPID!

A motorist had a flat tire in front of the insane asylum. He took the wheel off, and the bolts that held the wheel on rolled down into the sewer.

An inmate, looking through the fence, suggested that the man take one bolt from each of the remaining three wheels to hold the fourth wheel in place until he could get to a service station.

The motorist thanked him profusely and said, "I don't know why you are in that place."

The inmate said, "I'm here for being crazy, not for being stupid."

I'M SICK OF THIS

Nobody is sicker than the man who is sick on his day off.

I'M TIRED

I just found out why I feel tired all the time: We made a survey and found I was doing more than my share of the world's work.

The population of the country is 160 million, but there are 62 million people over 60 years of age. That leaves 98 million to do the work. People under 21 years of age total 54 million, which leaves 44 million to do the work.

Then there are 21 million who are employed by the government, and that leaves 23 million to do the work. Ten million are in the Armed Forces—that leaves 13 million to do the work. Now deduct 12,800,000—the number in state and city offices—and that leaves 200,000 to do the work. There are 126,000 in hospitals, insane asylums, and so forth—that leaves 74,000 people to do the work.

But 62,000 of these refuse to work, so that leaves 12,000 to do the work. Now it may interest you to know that there are 11,988 people in jail, so that leaves just *two* people to do all the work and that's *you* and *me* and I'm getting tired doing everything myself.

IDEA

"I've got an idea."
"Be kind to it. It's a long way from home."

THE IDEAL HUSBAND

What Every Woman Expects:

He will be a brilliant conversationalist.

He will be very sensitive, kind, understanding, truly loving.

He will be a very hardworking man.

He will help around the house by washing dishes, vacuuming floors, and taking care of the yard.

He will help his wife raise the children.

He will be a man of emotional and physical strength.

He will be as smart as Einstein, but will look like Robert Redford.

What She Gets:

He always takes her to the best restaurants. (Someday he may even take her inside.)

He doesn't have any ulcers—he gives them.

Anytime he gets an idea in his head, he has the whole thing in a nutshell.

He's well-known as a miracle worker—it's a miracle when he works.

He supports his wife in the manner to which she was accustomed—he's letting her keep her job.

He's such a bore that he even bores you to death when he gives you a compliment.

He has occasional flashes of silence that make his conversation brilliant.

IDEAL PREACHER

He preaches exactly 20 minutes and then sits down. He condemns sin, but never hurts anyone's feelings. He works from 8:00 A.M. to 10:00 P.M. in every type of work, from preaching to taxi service. He makes 60 dollars a week, wears good clothes, buys good books regularly, has a nice family, drives a good car, and gives 30 dollars a week to the church. He also stands ready to contribute to every good work that comes along. He is 26 years old and has been preaching for 30 years. He is tall and short, thin and heavyset, plain-looking but handsome. He has one brown eye and one blue, hair parted in the middle, left side straight and dark, the other side wavy and blond. He has a burning desire to work with teenagers, and spends all his time with the older folks. He smiles all the time with a straight face because he has a sense of humor that keeps him seriously dedicated to his work.

He makes 15 calls a day on church members, spends all his time evangelizing the unchurched, and is never out of his office. He is truly a remarkable person...and he does not exist.

IDEAL WIFE

WHAT EVERY MAN EXPECTS:

She will always be beautiful and cheerful. She could marry a movie star, but wants only you.

She will have hair that never needs curlers or beauty shops.

Her beauty won't run in a rainstorm.

She will never be sick—just allergic to jewelry and fur coats.

She will insist that moving the furniture by herself is good for her figure.

She will be an expert in cooking, cleaning house, fixing the car or TV, painting the house, and keeping quiet.

Her favorite hobbies will be mowing the lawn and shoveling snow.

She will hate charge cards.

Her favorite expression will be, "What can I do for you, Dear?"

She will think you have Einstein's brain but look like Mr. America.

She will wish you would go out with the boys so she could get some sewing done.

She will love you because you're so sexy.

WHAT HE GETS:

She speaks 140 words a minute, with gusts up to 180.

She was once a model for a totem pole.

She is a light eater—as soon as it gets light, she starts eating.

Where there's smoke, there she is—cooking.

She lets you know you only have two faults—everything you say and everything you do.

No matter what she does with it, her hair looks like an explosion in a steel wool factory.

If you get lost, open your wallet—she'll find you.

IDEAS

The reason ideas die quickly in some people's heads is because they can't stand solitary confinement.

IDIOT

"When I was a child I used to bite my fingernails; and the doctor told me if I didn't quit it I'd grow up to be an idiot."

"And you couldn't stop, huh?"

IMAGE

Mother: The baby is the image of his father.
Neighbor: What do you care, so long as he is healthy?

IMAGINARY

Teacher: What is the axis of the earth?
Student: The axis of the earth is an imaginary line which passes from one pole to the other, and on which the earth revolves.
Teacher: Very good. Now, could you hang clothes on that line?
Student: Yes, Sir.
Teacher: Indeed, and what sort of clothes?
Student: Imaginary clothes, Sir.

IMMATURE

One young mother, on receiving a nursery school report that described her daughter as "emotionally immature," asked with good sense, "If you can't be immature at three, when can you be?"

IMPROVE

Of all the awkward people in your house, there is only one you can improve very much.

INCOME TAX

Did you hear about the man from the income-tax bureau who phoned a certain Baptist minister to say, "We're checking the tax return of a member of your church, Deacon X, and notice he lists a donation to your building fund of 300 dollars. Is that correct?"

The minister answered without hesitation, "I haven't got my records available, but I'll promise you one thing: If he hasn't, he will!"

*　　*　　*

Don't be surprised if your next income-tax form is simplified to contain only four lines:
1. What was your income last year?
2. What were your expenses?
3. How much do you have left?
4. Send it in.

INDIAN

Clerk: This jug was made by a real Indian.

Elmer: But it says here it's made in Cleveland, Ohio.

Clerk: Well, didn't you ever hear of the Cleveland Indians?

INFLATION

Son: Dad, what is "creeping inflation"?

Father: It's when your mother starts out asking for new shoes and ends up with a complete new outfit.

INGRATITUDE

My brother was sort of odd. I remember once on his birthday he fell down a dry well, so we lowered his birthday cake to him. He didn't even tug on the rope to say thanks.

INSANE

A modern murderer is supposed to be innocent until he is proven insane.

*　　*　　*

An important official who was visiting an insane asylum made a telephone call but had difficulty getting his number. Finally, in exasperation, he shouted to the operator, "Look here, girl, do you know who I am?"

"No," she replied calmly, "but I know where you are."

INSANITY

Science has found that insanity is hereditary—parents get it from their children.

*　　*　　*

"Who is that strange-looking man who keeps staring at me?"

"Oh, that is Mr. Marconi, the famous expert on insanity."

INSECURE

Mother of small boy to child psychiatrist: "Well, I don't know whether or not he feels insecure, but everybody else in the neighborhood certainly does!"

INSOMNIA

"Do you know of any cures for insomnia?"
"Try talking to yourself."

INSURANCE

Jack: Don't you know that you can't sell insurance without a license?
Buck: I knew I wasn't selling any, but I didn't know the reason.

*   *   *

The following quotations were taken from a Toronto newspaper. They are samples of comments that individuals wrote down on their claim forms following their auto accidents.

- I misjudged a lady crossing the street.
- Coming home, I drove into the wrong house and collided with a tree I don't have.

- I collided with a stationary streetcar coming the opposite direction.

- The other car collided with mine without giving warning of its intentions.

- I heard a horn blow and was struck in the back—a lady was evidently trying to pass me.

- I thought my window was down, but found it was up when I put my hand through it.

- My car was stolen and sent up a human cry, but it has not been recovered.

- I collided with a stationary truck coming the other way.

- The truck backed through my windshield into my wife's face.

- A pedestrian hit me and went under my car.

- The guy was all over the road. I had to swerve a number of times before I hit him.

- If the other driver had stopped a few yards behind himself, the accident would not have happened.

- In my attempt to kill a fly, I drove into a telephone pole.

- I had been shopping for plants all day, and was on my way home. As I reached an intersection, a hedge sprang up, obscuring my vision. I did not see the other car.

- I had been driving my car for 40 years when I fell asleep at the wheel and had an accident.

- I was on my way to the doctor's with rear-end trouble when my universal joint gave way, causing me to have an accident.
- My car was legally parked as it backed into the other vehicle.
- An invisible car came out of nowhere, struck my vehicle, and vanished.
- I told the police that I was not injured, but on removing my hat, I found that I had a skull fracture.
- I was sure the old fellow would never make it to the other side of the roadway when I struck him.
- The pedestrian had no idea which way to go, so I ran over him.
- The indirect cause of this accident was a little guy in a small car with a big mouth.
- I was thrown from my car as it left the road. I was later found in a ditch by some stray cows.
- The telephone pole was approaching fast. I was attempting to swerve out of its path when it struck my front end.
- I was unable to stop in time, and my car crashed into the other vehicle. The driver and passengers then left immediately for a vacation with injuries.
- I pulled away from the side of the road, glanced at my mother-in-law, and headed over the embankment.

INTELLIGENCE

Two men were digging a ditch on a very hot day.

One said to the other, "Why are we down in this hole digging a ditch when our boss is standing up there under the shade of a tree?"

"I don't know," responded the other. "I'll ask him." So he climbed out of the hole and went to his boss. "Why are we digging in the hot sun and you are standing in the shade?"

"Intelligence," the boss said.

"What do you mean, 'intelligence'?"

The boss said, "Well, I'll show you. I'll put my hand on this tree and I want you to hit it with your fist as hard as you can." The ditchdigger took a mighty swing and tried to hit the boss' hand. The boss removed his hand and the ditchdigger hit the tree. The boss said, "That's intelligence!"

The ditchdigger went back to his hole. His friend asked, "What did he say?"

"He said we are down here because of intelligence."

"What's intelligence?" said the friend.

The ditchdigger put his hand on his face and said, "Take your shovel and hit my hand."

INTENSE ACTIVITY

Melba: I notice by this article that men become bald much more than women because of the intense activity of their brains.

Ken: Yes, and I notice that women don't grow beards because of the intense activity of their chins!

INTERRUPT

Member to pastor at the end of the morning

service: "Pastor, you were really good this morning! You interrupted my thoughts at least half a dozen times!"

INTRODUCTION

Recently our speaker had to discontinue several of his long talks on account of his throat. Several people threatened to cut it.

*   *   *

You have heard it said before that this speaker needs no introduction. Well, I have heard him and he needs all the introduction he can get.

*   *   *

You haven't heard nothing until you've heard our speaker of the evening. Then you've heard nothing.

*   *   *

As master of ceremonies, I am not going to stand up here and tell you a lot of old jokes. Our speaker, Mr. _____, will do that for me.

*   *   *

Our speaker needs no introduction. What he needs is a conclusion.

*   *   *

Tonight I would like to present to you _____ of whom the President of the United States once said: "Who?"

* * *

Our speaker will not bore you with a long speech—he can do it with a short one.

* * *

It is said that _____ is the greatest speaker in the business. And tonight we honor the man who made that statement, _____.

* * *

At the place our speaker last spoke, he drew a line three blocks long. But then the police took his chalk away.

* * *

I'm sorry to announce we have two disappointments tonight. Robert Redford couldn't make it, and _____ could.

* * *

You've been a wonderful audience—you stayed.

* * *

Our speaker for the evening gives the most refreshing talks. Everywhere he goes the audiences always feel good when they wake up.

* * *

This is a return speaking engagement for me. I was here 22 years ago.

INVENTOR

Did you hear about the inventor that came up with a knife that would slice two loaves of bread at the same time? He sold it to a large bakery. He then developed a knife that could slice three loaves of bread at the same time. He sold that idea, too!

Finally, the ultimate. He made a huge knife that could cut four loaves of bread at the same time! And so was born the world's first four-loaf cleaver.

IQ

He had an extremely high IQ when he was five. Too bad he grew out of it.

* * *

I wish I had a lower IQ so I could enjoy your company.

IRS

April is always a difficult month for Americans.

Even if your ship comes in, the IRS is right there to help you unload it.

* * *

IRS agent to taxpayer: "I'm afraid we can't allow you to deduct last year's tax as a bad investment."

* * *

"What kind of work do you do?"
"I work for the Bureau of Internal Revenue."
"Doesn't everybody?"

* * *

A businessman who was near death asked that his remains be cremated and the ashes be mailed to the Internal Revenue Service with the following note attached: "Now You Have It All."

IS THIS PIG?

A newly-married couple were entertaining, and among the guests was a man whose conduct was rather boisterous. At dinner he held up on his fork a piece of meat and in a vein of intended humor asked, "Is this pig?"

"To which end of the fork do you refer?" asked a quiet-looking man at the other end of the table.

THE ISMS

COMMUNISM: If you have two cows, you give both cows to the government, and then the government sells you some of the milk.

SOCIALISM: If you have two cows, you give both cows to the government, and then the government gives you some of the milk.

NAZISM: If you have two cows, the government shoots you and takes both cows.

FASCISM: If you have two cows, you milk both of them and give the government half of the milk.

NEW DEALISM: If you have two cows, you kill one, milk the other, and pour the milk down the drain.

CAPITALISM: If you have two cows, you sell one cow and buy a bull.

IT'S FLOODED

Wife: Honey, I can't get the car started. I think it's flooded.

Husband: Where is it?

Wife: In the swimming pool.

Husband: It's flooded.

IT'S HIS PROBLEM

Wife: George! Come quickly! A wild tiger has just gone into mother's tent!

Husband: Well, he got himself into that mess; let him get out of it!

IT'S THE PLUMBER

Once upon a time there was a parrot who could say only three little words: "Who is it?" One day when the parrot was alone in the house, there was a loud knock on the door. "Who is it?" screeched the parrot.

"It's the plumber," the visitor responded.

"Who is it?" repeated the parrot.

"It's the plumber, I tell you," was the reply. "You called me to tell me your cellar was flooded."

Again the parrot called, "Who is it?"

By this time, the plumber became so angry that he fainted. A neighbor rushed over to see the cause of the commotion, and found that the visitor had died because of a heart attack. The neighbor looked at the man and said, "Who is it?"

The parrot answered, "It's the plumber!"

IT'S YOURS

A Texan was visiting Scotland, and every time his host would show him a sight he would say, "That's nothing! We've got the same thing in Texas, only better!"

Finally they arrived at Loch Lomond. The Texan said, "Well, you have one thing that we don't have in Texas. This is a pretty lake."

The host said, "Well, you could dig a pipeline from Texas under the ocean and into the lake. If you can suck as hard as you can blow, the lake is yours."

JELLO

He's a regular Rock of Jello.

JERK

A chauffeur-driven Cadillac pulled up in front of our auditorium...stopped with a jerk...and out came our speaker of the evening.

JOB

Father: My son just received his B.A.
Neighbor: I suppose now he'll be looking for a Ph.D.
Father: No, now he's looking for a J-O-B.

JOHN SMITH

John Smith happened to witness a minor holdup. In due time the police arrived, and one officer asked the witness his name.
"John Smith," said Smith.
"Cut the comedy," snapped the cop. "What's your real name?"
"All right," said Smith, "put me down as Winston Churchill."
"That's more like it," said the officer. "You can't fool me with that Smith stuff."

JUDGE

A lady was showing a church friend her

neighbor's wash through her back window. "Our neighbor isn't very clean. Look at those streaks on the wash!"

Replied her friend, "Those streaks aren't on your neighbor's wash. They're on your window."

JULIUS CAESAR

Psychiatrist: Congratulations, Sir, you're cured.
Patient: Some cure. Before I was Julius Caesar. Now I'm nobody.

KARATE

Wife: You both arrived at that cab at the same time. Why did you let him have it? Why didn't you stand up for your rights?
Husband: He needed it more than I did. He was late to his karate class.

KAYAK

Two Eskimos sitting in a kayak were chilly, but when they lit a fire in the craft it sank—proving once and for all that you can't have your kayak and heat it, too.

KIBITZER

All evening long four cardplayers had been pestered by a kibitzer. When he went out of the room for a moment, they hit on a plan to silence him. "Let's make up a game no one ever heard of," one of them said. "Then he'll have to shut up."

The kibitzer returned. The dealer tore two cards in half and gave them to the man on his left. He tore the corners off three cards and spread them out in front of the man opposite him. Then he tore five cards in quarters, gave 15 pieces to the man on his right and kept five himself. "I have a mingle," he said. "I'll bet a dollar."

"I have a snazzle," the next man announced. "I'll raise you a dollar."

The third man folded without betting. The fourth, after due deliberation, said, "I've got a farfle. I'll raise you two dollars."

The kibitzer shook his head vehemently. "You're crazy," he said. "You're never going to beat a mingle and a snazzle with a lousy farfle!"

KICK IN THE PANTS

Dad: How dare you kick your little brother in the stomach!

Son: It's his own fault, Daddy. He turned around.

KIDS

Children would all be brought up perfectly if

families would just swap kids. Everyone knows what ought to be done with the neighbor's kids.

*   *   *

One nice thing about kids is that they don't keep telling you boring stories about the clever things their parents said.

KING

A lion was walking through the jungle taking a poll to determine who was the greatest among all the wild animals. When he saw the hippopotamus, he inquired, "Who is king of the jungle?"

"You are," said the hippopotamus.

Next he met a giraffe. "Who is king of the jungle?" he inquired.

"You are," said the giraffe.

Then he met a tiger and said, "Who is king of the jungle?"

"Oh, you are," said the tiger.

Finally he met an elephant. He gave him a good rap on the knee and said, "And who is king of the jungle?"

The elephant picked him up in his trunk and swung him against a large tree. As the lion bounced off the tree and hit the ground, he got up and dusted himself off and said, "You don't have to get so mad just because you don't know the right answer."

KING HEROD

During a seminary class, the lesson centered on the problem of King Herod offering up half his kingdom to see the daughter of Herodias dance.

"Now, what if you had this problem and you made the offer of anything she wanted and the girl came to you asking for the head of John the Baptist, and you didn't want to give her the head of John. What would you do?" asked the professor.

Soon a hand was raised. "I'd tell her," said one student, "that the head of John the Baptist was not in the half of the kingdom I was offering to her."

KIPPER

For many years a certain white whale and a tiny herring had been inseparable friends. Wherever the white whale roamed in search of food, the herring was sure to be swimming right along beside him.

One fine spring day the herring turned up off the coast of Norway without his companion. Naturally all the other fish were curious, and an octopus finally asked the herring what happened to his whale friend.

"How should I know?" the herring replied. "Am I my blubber's kipper?"

KISS

He: I promise you, the next time you contradict me, I'm going to kiss you.

She: Oh no you're not!

*   *   *

Bill: Am I the only man you ever have kissed?

Sue: Yes, and by far the best-looking.

*   *   *

Stealing a kiss may be petty larceny, but sometimes it's grand.

*   *   *

A man entered a bank with a gun in his hand. He bellowed, "I'm going to rob every man in this bank, and I'm going to kiss every woman."

One of the men who had accompanied his wife to the bank said, "You may rob all of us men, but you're not going to kiss all the ladies!"

His wife punched him in the ribs and said, "Now leave him alone, George. He's robbing the bank."

KISSING

A kiss is a peculiar proposition—of no use to one, yet absolute bliss to two. The small boy gets it for nothing, the young man has to lie for it, and the old man has to buy it. It is the baby's right, the lover's privilege, and the hypocrite's mask. To a young girl, it shows faith; to a married woman, hope; and to an old maid, charity.

KNITTING

Son: Why do the ladies always bring their knitting when they come to visit?

Father: So they will have something to think about while they talk.

LANGUAGE

Q. What's more clever than speaking in several languages?

A. Keeping your mouth shut in one.

LARGE RED COW

A man's car stalled on a country road. When he got out to fix it, a cow came along and stopped beside him. "Your trouble is probably in the carburetor," said the cow.

Startled, the man jumped back and ran down the road until he met a farmer. He told the farmer his story.

"Was it a large red cow with a brown spot over the right eye?" asked the farmer.

"Yes, yes," the man replied.

"Oh! I wouldn't listen to Bessie," said the farmer. "She doesn't know anything about cars."

THE LAST LAPP

If you're traveling in Scandinavia and you come to the last Lapp, you must be near the Finnish line.

LAST RESORT

I just heard of a man who met his wife at a travel bureau. She was looking for a vacation and he was the last resort.

THE LAST STRAW

Guest: What on earth do you put in your mattresses?

Innkeeper: The finest straw, Sir.

Guest: Now I know where the straw that broke the camel's back came from.

LAST WORDS

"Have you any last words," the warden asked the condemned man, "before we hang you?"

"Yes," panted the prisoner, "just get it over with quickly, please!"

The warden patted the man on the back, gave the signal, and the condemned man was dropped through the platform. But he didn't die—he kept bouncing up and down. So they drew him up and dropped him again. But still he didn't die—he just bounced up and down. Spectators began to faint as they heard the prisoner gasp, "C'mon and get through with this!"

So they lifted him up again and dropped him again, and once more he bobbed up and down at the end of the rope. The executioner was in a cold sweat and the guards had all they could do to keep the warden from passing out. When they drew him up for the eleventh time, the prisoner, eyeballs popping and tongue lolling out the side of his mouth, demanded, "C'mon and get through with this! What am I—a murderer or a yo-yo?"

LATE TO WORK

Every day Mr. Smith's secretary was 20 minutes late. Then one day she slid snugly into place only five minutes tardy.

"Well," said Mr. Smith, "This is the earliest you've ever been late."

LAWN MOWER

Wife: I'm happy to see that the neighbors finally returned our lawn mower before they moved. They certainly had it long enough.

Husband: *Our* lawn mower? I just bought it at the garage sale they're having.

LAWYER

My son, a lawyer, was approached by his friend, a priest, who wanted a will drawn up. When the work was completed and ready to be mailed, my son couldn't resist inserting this note: "Thy Will Be Done."

LEFTOVERS

The lady said to the waitress, "May I have a bag to carry leftovers to my dog?"

Her six-year-old said: "Oh Mother, are we going to get a dog?"

LET ME OUT

At a lecture series a very poor speaker was on the platform. As he was speaking, people in the audience began to get up and leave. After about ten minutes there was only one man left. Finally the man stopped speaking and asked the man why he remained to the end. "I'm the next speaker," was the reply.

LET'S MAKE A DEAL

A farmer and his wife went to a fair. The farmer was fascinated by the airplane rides, but he balked at the ten-dollar tickets.

"Let's make a deal," said the pilot. "If you and your wife can ride without making a single sound, I won't charge you anything. Otherwise you pay the ten dollars."

"Good deal!" said the farmer.

So they went for a ride. When they got back the pilot said, "If I hadn't been there, I never would have believed it. You never made a sound!"

"It wasn't easy, either," said the farmer. "I almost yelled when my wife fell out."

LET'S PLAY

Let's play horse. I'll be the front end...you just be yourself.

LETTER

Suddenly called out of town, a news commentator told his new secretary: "Write Allis-Chalmers in Milwaukee. Say that I can't keep that appointment Friday. I'm off for Texas. I'll telephone when I get back. Sign my name."

Upon his return, he found this carbon waiting:

Alice Chalmers
Milwaukee, Wisconsin

Dear Alice:

I'm off for Texas and can't keep that date....

The man promptly phoned the tractor company and said, "I hope you haven't received a certain letter."

"Received it!" came the reply. "It's been on the bulletin board for three days!"

*   *   *

Letter from son at school:

Dear Dad,

Gue$$ what I need mo$t. That'$ right. $end it $oon.

> Be$t wi$he$,
> Jay

Reply:

Dear Jay,

NOthing ever happens here. We kNOw you like school. Write aNOther letter soon. Mom was asking about you at NOon.

NOw I have to say good-bye.

> Dad

LIES

The following will help you to identify lies that are often told:

• I'm only thinking of you, Dear. Meaning: I am now about to get a bit of my own back.

• I don't want to make you unhappy. Meaning: I will now repeat to you certain malicious gossip which will reduce you to sleepless misery.

• I'm bound to admit. Meaning: I will now confuse the main issue.

• I'm not one to criticize. Meaning: I shall now proceed to find fault with all you have done.

• I'm as broad-minded as anyone. Meaning: All my ideas on this subject are hopelessly out-of-date.

• I hope I know my place. Meaning: I am about to step right out of it and tell you a few home truths.

• I'm a tolerant sort of fellow. Meaning: I can't endure you for another moment and am now preparing to throw you out of the house.

LIFE BELT

An ocean liner was sinking and the captain yelled: "Does anybody know how to pray?"

A minister on board said, "I do."

"Good," said the captain. "You start praying. The rest of us will put on the life belts. We are one belt short."

LIGHTEN UP

He lights up a room when he leaves it.

LIKE A FROG

Little girl: Grandfather, make like a frog.

Grandfather: What do you mean, make like a frog?

Little girl: Mommy says we're going to make a lot of money when you croak!

LIMBURGER CHEESE

Did you hear about the garlic and Limburger

cheese diet? You don't lose any weight, but your friends will think you look thinner at a distance.

LINGUIST

"I hear your husband is a linguist."

"Yes, he speaks three languages...golf, football, and baseball."

LIST OF SINS

A minister told his congregation that there were 739 different sins. He already has received 73 requests for the list.

LITTLE

A man went to the psychiatrist and complained about feeling inferior because of his height. The psychiatrist reminded the short fellow about the great men in history, such as Napoleon and Lautrec, who were great men in spite of their height.

The little man felt completely cured after talking to the psychiatrist and everything would have worked out fine, but as he went out of the doctor's office a cat ate him.

LOAFERS

During an Army war game a commanding

officer's jeep got stuck in the mud. The C.O. saw some men lounging nearby and asked them to help him get unstuck.

"Sorry, Sir," said one of the loafers, "but we've been classified dead and the umpire said we couldn't contribute in any way."

The C.O. turned to his driver and said, "Go drag a couple of those dead bodies over here and throw them under the wheels to give us some traction."

LOAN

John: Lend me fifty.

Jack: I have only forty.

John: Well, then let me have the forty and you can owe me the ten.

LOCAL CALL

Did you hear about the Texan who was trying to make a phone call?

"Operator, how much does it cost to call New York?"

"Three dollars and seventy-five cents," replied the operator.

"Why, I can call hell and back for that much," said the Texan.

"Yes, Sir," said the operator, "that's a local call!"

LONELY HEARTS CLUB

A man sent his picture to the Lonely Hearts Club. The reply came back, "We're not that lonely."

LONG HAIR

A long-haired boy was trying to get into a swim club, but was stopped by the owner who tried to explain that for health reasons long-haired boys were prohibited from using the pool.

"Get a haircut, and you're welcome," said the owner.

"Some of history's greatest men had long hair," said the young man.

"Those are the rules."

"Moses had long hair."

"Moses can't swim in our pool, either."

LONG-WINDED

The new preacher, at his first service, had a pitcher of water and a glass on the pulpit. As he preached, he drank until the pitcher of water was completely gone.

After the service someone asked an old woman of the church, "How did you like the new pastor?"

"Fine," she said, "but he's the first windmill I ever saw that was run by water."

LOOPHOLE

On visiting a seriously ill lawyer in the hospital, his friend found him sitting up in bed, frantically leafing through the Bible.

"What are you doing?" asked the friend.

"Looking for loopholes," replied the lawyer.

LORD'S PRAYER

Two lawyers were bosom buddies. Much to the amazement of one, the other became a Sunday school teacher. "I bet you don't even know the Lord's Prayer," the first one fumed.

"Everybody knows that," the other replied. "It's 'Now I lay me down to sleep...'"

"You win," said the first one admiringly. "I didn't know you knew so much about the Bible."

LOVE

Better to have loved a short man than never to have loved a tall.

*　　*　　*

Guy: Margie, I love you! I love you, Margie!

Gal: In the first place, you don't love me; and in the second place, my name isn't Margie.

*　　*　　*

Love may be blind, but it seems to be able to find its way around in the dark.

*　　*　　*

Linda: Do you really love me, or do you just think you do?

Jack: Honey, I really love you. I haven't done any thinking yet.

*　　*　　*

Girl: Do you love me?
Boy: Yes, Dear.
Girl: Would you die for me?
Boy: No—mine is an undying love.

*　　*　　*

Love is sometimes like a poisoned mushroom. You can't tell if it's the real thing until it's too late.

*　　*　　*

Becky: Do you love me with all your heart and soul?
Dave: Uh-huh.
Becky: Do you think I'm the most beautiful girl in the world?
Dave: Uh-huh.
Becky: Do you think my lips are like rose petals?
Dave: Uh-huh.
Becky: Oh, you say the most beautiful things.

*　　*　　*

John: I can't seem to get anywhere with Jan.
Jack: What happened?
John: I told her I was knee-deep in love with her.

Jack: What was her reaction?

John: She promised to put me on her wading list.

LUCKY SAUCER

In front of a delicatessen, an art connoisseur noticed a mangy little kitten lapping up milk from a saucer. The saucer, he realized with a start, was a rare and precious piece of pottery.

He sauntered into the store and offered two dollars for the cat. "It's not for sale," said the proprietor.

"Look," said the collector, "that cat is dirty and undesirable, but I'm eccentric. I like cats that way. I'll raise my offer to five dollars."

"It's a deal," said the proprietor, and pocketed the five on the spot.

"For that sum I'm sure you won't mind throwing in the saucer," said the connoisseur. "The kitten seems so happy drinking from it."

"Nothing doing," said the proprietor firmly. "That's my lucky saucer. From that saucer, so far this week I've sold 34 cats."

LUNATICS

Son: How do they catch lunatics, Dad?

Dad: With lipstick, beautiful dresses, and pretty smiles.

LYING

A minister wound up the services one morning

by saying, "Next Sunday I am going to preach on the subject of liars. And in this connection, as a preparation for my discourse, I would like you all to read the seventeenth chapter of Mark." On the following Sunday, the preacher rose to begin, and said, "Now, then, all of you who have done as I requested and read the seventeenth chapter of Mark, please raise your hands." Nearly every hand in the congregation went up. Then said the preacher, "You are the people I want to talk to. There is no seventeenth chapter of Mark."

MAJOR DECISIONS

In my house, I make all the major decisions and my wife makes the minor ones. For example, I decide such things as East-West trade, crime in the streets, welfare cheating, and tax increases. My wife decides the minor things such as which house to buy, what kind of car we drive, how much money to spend, how to raise the children, etc.

MAKES SENSE TO ME

Employer: We can pay you 80 dollars a week now and 100 dollars a week in eight months.

Applicant: Thank you. I'll drop back in eight months.

MARBLEHEAD

"In Massachusetts they named a town after you."
"What is it?"
"Marblehead."

MARBLES

In order to become a good speaker, you must go
to diction school. They teach you how to speak
clearly. To do this, they fill your mouth with
marbles and you're supposed to talk clearly right
through the marbles. Now every day you lose one
marble. When you've lost all your marbles...

MARRIAGE

A couple's happy married life almost went on the
rocks because of the presence in the household of
old Aunt Emma. For seven long years she lived with
them, always crotchety, always demanding. Finally
the old girl died.

On the way back from the cemetery, the husband
confessed to his wife, "Darling, if I didn't love you
so much, I don't think I would have put up with
having your Aunt Emma in the house all those
years."

His wife looked at him aghast. "*My* Aunt
Emma!" she cried. "I thought she was *your* Aunt
Emma!"

* * *

Marriage is like a midnight phone call—you get a ring, and then you wake up.

*   *   *

Marriage is nature's way of keeping people from fighting with strangers.

*   *   *

Marriage is like a railroad sign—first you stop, then you look, then you listen.

MASKS

When I got the bill for my operation, I found out why they wear masks in the operating room.

MATHEMATICS

A Missouri farmer passed away and left 17 mules to his three sons. The instructions left in the will said that the oldest boy was to get one-half, the second eldest one-third, and the youngest one-ninth. The three sons, recognizing the difficulty of dividing 17 mules into these fractions, began to argue.

Their uncle heard about the argument, hitched up his mule, and drove out to settle the matter. He added his mule to the 17, making 18. The eldest son therefore got one-half or nine; the second got one-third or six; and the youngest got one-ninth or two. Adding up 9, 6, and 2 equals 17. The uncle, having settled the argument, hitched up his mule and drove home.

MAXED OUT

Max looked up at the steep, icy mountainside. "I can't do it," he said.

His companions begged him to climb the mountain with them, but he refused to move. "I'm against mountain climbing," he said.

Now they call him "Anti-climb-Max."

MAYFLOWER

"My folks came over on the Mayflower."

"Don't feel bad about it. We can't all be born here."

ME, TOO

A Texas rancher was visiting an Iowa farm. The Iowa farmer was justly proud of his 200 acres of rich, productive land.

"Is this your whole farm?" the Texan asked. "Why, back in Texas I get in my car at 5:00 in the morning, and I drive and drive all day. At dusk I just reach the end of my ranch."

The Iowa farmer thought a while and replied, "I used to have a car like that, too."

MEDICARE

A sample of what might happen if we had socialized medicine is currently making the rounds. It goes something like this:

A man, feeling the need of medical care, went to the medical building. Upon entering the front door, he found himself faced with a battery of doors, each marked with the names of ailments such as appendicitis, heart disease, cancer, etc.

He felt sure his trouble could be diagnosed as appendicitis, so he entered the door so marked. Upon entering, he found himself faced with two more doors, one marked male and the other female. He entered the door marked male and found himself in another corridor where there were two doors, one marked Protestant and the other Catholic.

Since he was a Protestant, he entered the proper door and found himself facing two more doors, one marked white and the other colored. He entered the white door and again was faced with two more doors marked taxpayer and nontaxpayer. He still owned equity in his home, so he went through the door marked taxpayer, and found himself confronted with two more doors marked single and married.

He had a wife at home, so he entered the proper door and once more there were two more doors, one marked Republican and the other Democrat.

Since he was a Republican he entered that door and fell nine floors to the alley.

MEDICINE

The doctor told me to take this medicine after a hot bath. I could hardly finish drinking the bath!

MELODY IN F (THE PRODIGAL SON)

Feeling footloose and frisky, a featherbrained fellow
Forced his fond father to fork over the farthings
And flew far to foreign fields
And frittered his fortune feasting fabulously with
   faithless friends.
Fleeced by his fellows in folly, and facing famine,
He found himself a feed-flinger in a filthy
   farmyard.
Fairly famishing, he fain would have filled his
   frame
With foraged food from fodder fragments.
"Phooey, my father's flunkies fare far finer,"
The frazzled fugitive forlornly fumbled, frankly
   facing facts.
Frustrated by failure, and filled with foreboding,
He fled forthwith to his family.
Falling at his father's feet, he forlornly fumbled,
"Father, I've flunked,
And fruitlessly forfeited family fellowship favor."
The farsighted father, forestalling further
   flinching,
Frantically flagged the flunkies to
Fetch a fatling from the flock and fix a feast.
The fugitive's faultfinding brother frowned

On fickle forgiveness of former folderol.
But the faithful father figured,
"Filial fidelity is fine, but the fugitive is found!
What forbids fervent festivity?
Let flags be unfurled! Let fanfares flare!"
Father's forgiveness formed the foundation
For the former fugitive's future fortitude!

MEMORY

A tourist was introduced to an Indian in New Mexico who was said to have a perfect memory. Skeptical, the tourist asked, "What did you have for breakfast on September 10, 1943?"

The Indian answered, "Eggs."

The man scoffed, "Everyone eats eggs for breakfast. He's a phony."

Thirteen years later the traveler's train stopped again in the small New Mexico town, and he saw the same Indian sitting on the train platform. The tourist went up to him and said jovially, "How!"

The Indian answered, "Scrambled."

MEMORY LOSS

There are three ways to tell if you are getting old: first, a loss of memory; second...

MENTAL BLOCK

A street on which several psychiatrists live.

MENTAL ILLNESS

The only reason we invited him here tonight is to remind you that every 60 seconds mental illness strikes!

MENTAL PATIENTS

When a busload of people entered a large restaurant, the leader of the group approached the manager.

"Sir, I'm Mr. Phillips of the Kingsview Mental Hospital. These nice folks are mental patients in our halfway house program. They've all been cured, but they do have one small problem: They will want to pay you in bottle caps. So if you'll be so kind as to humor them in this way, I'll take care of the bill when they are through."

The manager, wanting to be a good citizen, collected the bottle caps. The leader returned and with gratitude said, "Thank you so very much. I'll pay the bill now. Do you have change for a hubcap?"

MENTALLY ILL

One out of four Americans is mentally ill. Next time you're in a group of four people, take a good look at the other three. If they look all right, you're it!

METAL AGE

We live in the Metal Age:

Silver in the hair.
Gold in the teeth.
Lead in the pants.
Iron in the veins.

MIDDLE AGE

Middle age is when you know all the answers and nobody asks you the questions.

MIDGET

During the days of the Salem, Massachusetts, witch hunts, a midget was imprisoned for fortune-telling. She later escaped from jail, and the headline in the local newspaper read: SMALL MEDIUM AT LARGE.

MILLIONAIRE

A billionaire after taxes.

MIND

Jay: I have half a mind to get married.
Bob: That's all you need.

MIND READER

Melba: I can't decide whether to go to a palmist or to a mind reader.

Ken: Go to a palmist. It's obvious that you have a palm.

MINISTER

The new minister stood at the church door greeting the members as they left the Sunday morning service. Most of the people were very generous in telling the new minister how they liked his message, except for one man who said, "That was a very dull and boring sermon, Pastor."

In a few minutes the same man appeared again in line and said, "I don't think you did any preparation for your message, Pastor."

Once again, the man appeared, this time muttering, "You really blew it. You didn't have a thing to say, Pastor."

Finally the minister could stand it no longer. He went over to one of the deacons and inquired about the man.

"Oh, don't let that guy bother you," said the deacon. "He is a little slow. All he does is go around repeating whatever he hears other people saying."

* * *

A minister was asked to inform a man with a heart condition that he had just inherited a million dollars. Everyone was afraid the shock would cause a heart attack and the man would die.

The minister went to the man's house and said, "Joe what would you do if you inherited a million dollars?" Joe responded, "Well, Pastor, I think I would give half of it to the church."

The minister fell over dead.

MINOR OPERATION

A minor operation is one performed on somebody else.

MISERABLE

"You know, girls, a lot of men are going to be miserable when I marry."

"Really? How many men are you going to marry?"

MISJUDGED

Wife: I should have taken my mother's advice and never married you! How she tried to stop me!

Husband: Holy mackerel, how I've misjudged that woman!

MONEY TALK

Money talks...it says good-bye.

MONKEY

I haven't much doubt that man sprang from the monkey, but where did the monkey spring from?

MOODY

My husband has three moods: hungry, thirsty, or both.

MOONSHINE

The prosecution and defense had both presented their final arguments in a case involving a Kentucky moonshiner.

The judge turned to the jury and asked: "Before giving you your instructions, do any of you have any questions?"

"Yes, Your Honor," replied one of the jurors. "Did the defendant boil the malt one or two hours, does he cool it quickly, and at what point does he add the yeast?"

MORNING

If the Lord wanted us to enjoy sunrises, they would come at 10:00 in the morning.

MOSES

Teacher: You can be sure that if Moses were alive today, he'd be considered a remarkable man.

Lenny: He sure ought to be—he'd be more than 2,500 years old.

THE MOST DANGEROUS YEAR

The most dangerous year in married life is the

first. Then follows the second, third, fourth,
fifth...

MOTHER-IN-LAW

Did you hear about the man who was driving
down the street, when all of a sudden he came
across a long line of people. They were all walking
single file in the middle of the road. He drove past
100, then 200, then 300, until he lost count. All of
them were walking single file down the yellow line
in the center of the street.

Finally, up ahead he saw the line of people
slowing down to a standstill. At the head of the line
he saw a hearse, and then another hearse, and then
a big black limousine. The limousine had a flat tire
and the driver was changing the tire. The man's
curiosity was so great that he pulled his car over to
the side of the road, got out, walked over to the
limousine, and knocked on the window.

The window rolled down, and he saw a man in a
black suit, and next to him on the seat was a dog.
Finally, the man spoke to the fellow in the black
suit. "Pardon me, Sir," he said, "but I have never
seen a funeral like this before. Could you tell me
what is going on?"

The man in the suit replied, "Well, in the first
hearse is my wife. The dog sitting next to me killed
her."

"Oh, I'm terribly sorry," said the man. "But what
about the second hearse?"

The man in the suit said, "In the second hearse is my mother-in-law, and the dog next to me killed her also."

"I'm so sorry," said the man. He then started to walk back to his car. About halfway there, he turned around and went back to the limousine. He said, "Excuse me, Sir, but would it be possible to borrow your dog for awhile?"

The man in the black suit replied, "Get in line."

MOTHER'S DAY

Mother's Day brings back memories of maternal advice and admonition. Picture the scene with these famous offspring:

Alexander the Great's mother: "How many times do I have to tell you—you can't have everything you want in this world!"

Franz Schubert's mother: "Take my advice, Son. Never start anything you can't finish."

Achilles' mother: "Stop imagining things. There's nothing wrong with your heel."

Madame de Pompadour's mother: "For heaven's sake, child, do something about your hair!"

Sigmund Freud's mother: "Stop pestering me! I've told you a hundred times the stork brought you!"

MOTIVATION

A young man had a job with a company that required him to work very late at night. In going home after work, he found that it was fastest to walk through a cemetery near his home. One night when he was very tired, he accidentally fell into a freshly dug grave.

At first he was not too concerned, but when he realized that he could not get out because the hole was too deep, he became somewhat hysterical. Finally, in complete exhaustion, he sat down in the corner of the grave and fell asleep.

Shortly thereafter another man decided to walk through the cemetery and happened to fall into the same grave. He too went through great effort to get out but could not. He then moved around the grave until he stepped on the first man who was asleep. The first man woke up and shouted, "YOU CAN'T GET OUT OF HERE!"

But the second man did.

MOTORCYCLE

Two men were traveling on a motorcycle on a windy winter day. When it became too breezy for one, he stopped and put his overcoat on backwards to keep the wind from ballooning it away from him. A few miles further on, the motorcycle hit a tree, killing the driver and stunning the fellow with the reversed coat. Later, when the coroner visited the scene, he asked a rookie policeman standing nearby: "What happened?"

"Well," the officer replied, "one of them was dead when I got here, and by the time I got the head of the other one straightened around, he was dead, too."

MOUNTAINS

"The reason I climb mountains is because they are there!"

"That's the reason everybody else goes around them!"

MOUSE

Teacher: Robert Burns wrote "To a Field Mouse."

Student: I'll bet he didn't get an answer.

MOUSETRAP

Young wife: Don't forget to bring home another mousetrap.

Husband: What's the matter with the one I brought yesterday?

Young wife: It's full!

MOUTH FIRST

He is the only person who enters the room mouth first!

MOZART

A married couple trying to live up to a snobbish life-style went to a party. The conversation turned to Mozart. "Absolutely brilliant, magnificent, a genius!"

The woman, wanting to join in the conversation, remarked casually, "Ah, Mozart. You're so right. I love him. Only this morning I saw him getting on the No. 5 bus going to Coney Island." There was a sudden hush, and everyone looked at her. Her husband was mortified. He pulled her away and whispered, "We're leaving right now. Get your coat and let's get out of here."

As they drove home, he kept muttering to himself. Finally his wife turned to him. "You're angry about something."

"Oh really? You noticed?" he sneered. "I've never been so embarrassed in my life! You saw Mozart take the No. 5 bus to Coney Island? You idiot! Don't you know the No. 5 bus doesn't go to Coney Island?"

MUD HOLE

A motorist, after being bogged down in a muddy road, paid a passing farmer five dollars to pull him out with his tractor. After he was back on dry ground he said to the farmer, "At those prices, I should think you would be pulling people out of the mud night and day."

"Can't," replied the farmer. "At night I haul water for the hole."

MUD PACK

"Every once in awhile my wife puts on one of those mud packs."

"Does it improve her looks?"

"Only for a few days...then the mud falls off!"

MUD PIES

A man pleaded with the psychiatrist, "You've got to help me. It's my son."

"What's the matter?"

"He's always eating mud pies. I get up in the morning and there he is in the backyard eating mud pies. I come home at lunch and he is eating mud pies. I come home at dinner and there he is in the backyard eating mud pies."

The psychiatrist reassured him, "Give the kid a chance It's all part of growing up. It'll pass."

"Well, I don't like it, and neither does his wife."

MURDER

"Have you ever thought about divorcing your wife?"

"Divorce?...No. Murder?...Yes!"

MY FIRST

"Excuse me for being nervous," the sheriff apologized as he slipped the noose over the condemned man's head. "This is my first hanging."

"Mine too!" the condemned man replied.

MY GIRLFRIEND

Harry: My girlfriend has a huge lower lip, but I don't mind.

Gary: You don't?

Harry: No, her upper lip covers it!

MY LUCKY NUMBER

Thirteen ministers were on a flight to New York. When they came into a large storm, they told the stewardess to tell the pilot that everything would be okay because 13 ministers were on board.

Later the stewardess returned from the cockpit.

"What did the pilot say?" one preacher asked.

"He said he was glad to have 13 ministers aboard but he would rather have four good engines."

NEARSIGHTED

Jack: I'm so nearsighted I nearly worked myself to death.

Elmer: What's being nearsighted got to do with working yourself to death?

Jack: I couldn't tell whether the boss was watching me or not, so I had to work all the time.

NEIGHBORS

The only people who listen to both sides of an argument are the neighbors.

NERVE

Someone asked, "What is the most sensitive nerve in the human body?"

The preacher answered, "The one that leads to the pocketbook."

NERVES

The best way to cure your wife of a case of nerves is to tell her it's caused by advancing age.

NERVOUS BREAKDOWN

"To tell the truth, Doctor," said a hardworking housewife, "I've always wanted to have a nervous breakdown. But every time I was about to get around to it, it was time to fix somebody a meal."

NIBBLE

Wife: When we were younger, you used to nibble on my ear.

Husband: Excuse me. I'll be right back.
Wife: Where are you going?
Husband: I'm going to get my teeth.

NIGHT

Late-staying guest: Well, good night. I hope I have not kept you up too late.

Yawning host: Not at all. We would have been getting up soon, anyway.

NO BOTHER

"Don't bother showing me to the door."
"It's no bother...it's a pleasure!"

NO END

There are usually two sides to every argument, but no end.

NOBODY LIKES ME

The mother was having a hard time getting her son to go to school in the morning.

"Nobody in school likes me," he complained. "The teachers don't like me, the kids don't like me, the superintendent wants to transfer me, the bus drivers hate me, the school board wants me to drop out, and the custodians have it in for me. I don't want to go to school."

"But you have to go to school," countered his mother. "You are healthy, you have a lot to learn, you have something to offer others, you are a leader. And besides, you are 45 years old and you are the principal."

NONCONFORMIST

A man entered a barbershop and said: "I am tired of looking like everyone else! I want a change! Part my hair from ear to ear!"

"Are you sure?"

"Yes!" said the man.

The barber did as he was told, and a satisfied customer left the shop.

Three hours passed and the man reentered the shop. "Put it back the way it was," he said.

"What's the matter?" said the barber. "Are you tired of being a nonconformist already?"

"No," he replied, "I'm tired of people whispering in my nose!"

NORMAL DEATH

Every chair in the doctor's waiting room was filled and some patients were standing. At one point the conversation died down and there was silence. During the silence an old man stood up wearily and remarked, "Well, guess I'll go home and die a natural death."

NOSTRIL

She has long, flowing blonde hair...from each nostril.

NOT BAD

"How long have you two been married?" asked a friend.

"We've been happily married for seven years," answered the husband. "Seven out of 16 isn't bad."

NOT HERE

Joe and Bill met on a street corner. When Joe said he sure was glad to see his friend, Bill answered, "How can you see me when I'm not even here? And I'll bet you ten dollars I can prove it!"

"You're going to bet me ten dollars you're not here? Okay, it's a bet. Go ahead and prove it."

"Am I in Chicago?"

"Nope."

"Am I in New York?"

Joe answered emphatically, "No!"

"Well, if I'm not in Chicago and I'm not in New York, that means I'm in some other place, right?"

"That's right."

"Well, if I'm in some other place, I can't be here. I'll take that ten dollars."

"How can I give you the money if you're not here?"

NOTE

The following note was fastened to a defective parking meter with a rubber band:

"I put three nickels in this meter. License number 4761PQ."

"FRD719—Me, too!"

"So did I—JRY335."

"I'm not going to pay a nickel to find out if these guys are lying. WTM259."

NOTES

A minister preached a very short sermon. He explained, "My dog got into my office and chewed up some of my notes."

At the close of the service a visitor asked, "If your dog ever has pups, please let my pastor have one of them."

NOTHING

Most of us know how to say nothing...few of us know when.

*   *   *

A pastor, burdened by the importance of his work, went into the sanctuary to pray. Falling to his knees, he lamented, "O Lord, I am nothing! I am nothing!"

The minister of education passed by and, overhearing the prayer, was moved to join the pastor on his knees. Shortly he, too, was crying aloud, "O Lord, I too am nothing. I am nothing."

The janitor of the church, awed by the sight of the two men praying, joined them, crying, "O Lord, I also am nothing. I am nothing."

At this, the minister of education nudged the pastor and said, "Now look who thinks he's nothing!"

NOTHING'S WRONG

The airline company was disturbed over a high percentage of accidents, and decided to eliminate human errors by building a completely mechanical plane.

"Ladies and gentlemen," came a voice over a loudspeaker on the maiden voyage, "it may interest you to know that you are now traveling in the world's first completely automatic plane. Now just sit back and relax because nothing can possibly go wrong...go wrong...go wrong...go wrong..."

NUDITY

Phyllis Diller says there's so much nudity in films that this year's Oscar for clothing design will probably go to a dermatologist.

NUMBERS

If the metric system ever takes over we may have to say the following:

• A miss is as good as 1.6 kilometers.

• Put your best 0.3 of a meter forward.

• Spare the 5.03 meters and spoil the child.

• Twenty-eight grams of prevention is worth 453 grams of cure.

• Give a man 2.5 centimeters and he'll take 1.6 kilometers.

• Peter Piper picked 8.8 liters of pickled peppers.

NUTS TO YOU

A pastor got this note addressed to him and his wife accompanying a box of goodies from an old lady in the parish:

"Dear Pastor: Knowing that you do not eat sweets, I am sending candy to your wife—and nuts to you."

OFF AND RUNNING

Two men went to the train station with a friend. The train was late, so they sat down for a cup of coffee. They talked and drank and forgot about the train. Suddenly they heard the last announcement about the departing train. They all got up and started running. They ran down the tracks as the train was pulling out of the station. Two of the men just made it to the last car and the third man was not quite fast enough. The third man slowed to a stop and started laughing. An onlooker went up to the laughing man and said, "What are you laughing for? You just missed your train."

"You're right," was the reply. "I did miss my train. What's funny is that those two men came to see me off."

OFF WITH YOUR HEAD!

Did you hear about the count who stole the king's crown? They tried and tried to make him confess, but he would not. Finally, they said, "We will chop off your head if you don't tell us." He wouldn't tell them, so they took him to the chopping block. They told him that he would have one more chance but he did not take it. As the head chopper started down with the ax, the count said, "All right, I'll tell you." It was too late...his head went rolling to the ground.

Moral: Don't hesitate your counts before they chicken.

OFFERING

An usher was passing the collection plate at a large church wedding. One of those attending looked up, very puzzled. Without waiting for the question, the usher nodded his head and said, "I know it's unusual, but the father of the bride requested it."

OFFICE

Husband (Reading the morning paper): Another cup of coffee!

Wife: Aren't you going to the office today?

Husband: Oh, my goodness. I thought I was at the office!

OH, BOY

"This house," said the real estate salesman, "has both its good points and its bad points. To show you I'm honest, I'm going to tell you about both. The disadvantages are that there is a chemical plant one block south and a slaughterhouse a block north."

"What are the advantages?" inquired the prospective buyer.

"The advantage is that you can always tell which way the wind is blowing."

OH, MY ACHING BACK

As they left the auditorium after a two-hour lecture on nineteenth-century English poets, the wife exclaimed, "Didn't it make your mind soar?"

"Yes," her husband agreed grimly, "and my backside, too!"

OKAY

A little boy never said a word for six years. One day his parents served him cocoa. From out of left field the kid said, "This cocoa's no good."

His parents went around raving. They asked him, "Why did you wait so long to talk?"

He said, "Up till now everything's been okay."

OLD AGE

You are getting old when your back goes out more often than you do.

OLD BORE

A tired minister was at home resting, and through the window he saw a woman approaching his door. She was one of those too-talkative people, and he was not anxious to talk with her. He said to his wife, "I'll just duck upstairs and wait until she goes away."

An hour passed, then he tiptoed to the stair landing and listened—not a sound. He was very pleased, so he started down calling loudly to his wife, "Well, My Dear, did you get rid of that old bore at last?"

The next moment he heard the voice of the same woman caller, and she couldn't possibly have missed hearing him. Two steps down, he saw them both staring up at him. It seemed truly a crisis moment.

The quick-thinking minister's wife answered, "Yes, Dear, she went away over an hour ago. But Mrs. Jones has come to call in the meantime, and I'm sure you'll be glad to greet her."

OLD FAITHFUL

He: Where are you going on your vacation?
Him: Yellowstone National Park.
He: Don't forget Old Faithful.
Him: She's going with me.

OLD NATURE

A man was taken to court for stealing an item from a store. The man said to the judge, "Your Honor, I'm a Christian. I've become a new man. But I have an old nature also. It was not my new man who did wrong. It was my old man."

The judge responded, "Since it was the old man that broke the law, we'll sentence him to 60 days in jail. And since the new man was an accomplice in the theft, we'll give him 30 days, too. I therefore sentence you both to 90 days in jail."

OLD PROVERB

Bob: Don't be afraid of my dog. You know the old proverb, "A barking dog never bites."

Rich: Yes, you know the proverb, and I know the proverb, but does your dog know the proverb?

OLDER

You can tell you are getting older when:

• You sit in a rocking chair and can't get it going.

• You burn the midnight oil after 8:00 P.M.

• You look forward to a dull evening.

• Your knees buckle and your belt won't.

• Your little black book contains only names ending in M.D.

• You decide to procrastinate and never get around to it.

• Dialing long distance wears you out.

• You walk with your head held high, trying to get used to your bifocals.

• You sink your teeth into a steak and they stay there.

OLD-TIMER

One who remembers when people who wore blue jeans worked.

*   *   *

You are an old-timer if you remember when a baby-sitter was called Mother.

*   *   *

You're an old-timer if you remember when the only babes politicians kissed were those in their mother's arms.

ONLY A DIME

A man entered a barbershop and asked for a shave. After the shave, the barber said, "That will be ten cents, please."

"But," said the man, "your sign says $1.25 for a shave. How come only ten cents?"

The barber answered, "Once in awhile we get a guy that is all mouth and we only charge him a dime!"

OOPS

Customer: I am sorry, Waiter, but I only have enough money for the bill. I have nothing left for a tip.

Waiter: Let me add up that bill again, Sir.

OPEN MIND

You really have an open mind...and a mouth to match.

OPEN MOUTH—INSERT FOOT

A small man said to a large man, "If I were as big as you, I would go into the jungle, find me a big lion, and pull him limb from limb."

The big man replied, "There are some little lions in the jungle, too. Let's see what you can do."

OPERATION

Q. What is the greatest surgical operation on record?
A. Lancing Michigan.

OPPORTUNITY

The trouble with opportunity is that it's always more recognizable going than coming.

OPPOSITES

Your Problem/My Situation

When you get angry it is because you are ill-tempered./It just happens that my nerves are bothering me.

When you don't like someone it is because you are prejudiced./I happen to be a good judge of human nature.

When you compliment someone it is because you use flattery./I only encourage folks.

When you take a long time to do a job it is because you are unbearably slow and pokey./When I take a long time it is because I believe in quality workmanship.

When you spend your paycheck in 24 hours, it is because you are a spendthrift./When I do, it is because I am generous.

When you stay in bed until 11 A.M., it is because you are a lazy good-for-nothing./When I stay in bed a little longer, it is because I am totally exhausted.

OPTIMIST

The optimist fell from the top story of a skyscraper. As he passed the tenth story, he was overheard muttering: "So far, so good!"

OUR FATHER

Pilot: Pilot to tower...pilot to tower...I am 300 miles from land...600 feet high and running out of gas...please instruct...over.

Tower: Tower to pilot...tower to pilot...repeat after me...Our Father, which art in heaven...

OUT OF AFRICA

Boy: Do you know, Dad, that in some parts of Africa a man doesn't know his wife until he marries her?

Dad: Why single out Africa?

OUT OF GAS

A boy and a girl were out driving one evening.

They came to a quiet spot on a country lane, and the car stopped. "Out of gas," said the boy.
The girl opened her purse and pulled out a bottle.
"Wow!" said the boy. "A bottle...what is it?"
"Gasoline," said the girl.

PAIN IN THE NECK

The man who thinks he knows it all is a pain in the neck to those of us who really do.

*   *   *

"How is the pain in your neck?"
"He's out playing golf."

PANCAKES

The sad, quiet, big-eyed little lady sat in the psychiatrist's office. The good doctor questioned her gently as to why her family wanted her locked up.

"Now, tell me," he said, "just what your trouble is."

"It's just that...just that I'm so fond of pancakes, Doctor."

"Is that all? Why, I'm very fond of pancakes myself."

"Oh Doctor, really? You must come over to our house. I've got trunks and trunks full of them!"

PARACHUTE JUMP

Just before a drafted farm boy made his first

parachute jump, his sergeant reminded him, "Count to ten and pull the first rip cord. If it snarls, pull the second rip cord for the auxiliary chute. After you land, our truck will pick you up."

The paratrooper took a deep breath and jumped. He counted to ten, and pulled the first cord. Nothing happened. He pulled the second cord. Again, nothing happened. As he careened crazily earthward, he said to himself: "Now I'll bet that truck won't be there either!"

PARDON

"I beg your pardon for coming so late."

"My Dear, no pardons are needed. You can never come too late."

PARENTS

I've wanted to run away from home more often since I've had kids than when I was a boy.

PARROT

A dignified old clergyman owned a parrot of which he was exceedingly fond, but the bird had picked up an appalling vocabulary of cuss words from a previous owner and, after a series of embarrassing episodes, the clergyman decided he would have to kill his pet. A lady in his parish suggested a last-ditch remedy. "I have a female parrot," she said, "who is an absolute saint. She sits quietly on her perch and says nothing but 'Let's pray.' Why don't you bring your parrot over and see if my own bird's good influence doesn't reform him?"

The clergyman said it was worth a trial, and the next night he arrived with his pet tucked under his arm. The bird took one look at the lady parrot and chirped, "Hi, Toots. How about a little kiss?"

"My prayers have been answered," said the lady parrot gleefully.

PARTING

Two partners had come to the parting of the ways over social and business differences.

"You stole my accounts," shouted one. "You crook."

"And you stole my wife," shouted the other. "You horse thief."

PASTOR

An elderly woman was weeping as she bade good-bye to the man who had been pastor of her church for several years.

"My dear lady," consoled the departing pastor, "don't get so upset. The bishop surely will send a much better pastor to replace me here."

"That's what they told us the last time," wailed the woman.

PAYMENT

A customer was several months behind in paying his bill, and his last payment notice informed him that he would have to pay or the matter would be turned over to a lawyer. He responded with the following note: "Enclosed you will find a check for the entire amount. Please forgive my delay in not answering sooner. Thank you for your patience. I remain, Yours truly..."

"P.S. This is the kind of a letter I would write to you if I had the money to pay."

PEARLS

Interrupted by the sound of the bell announcing the end of the class, the professor was annoyed to see the students noisily preparing to leave although he was in the middle of his lecture. "Just a moment, Gentlemen," he said, "I have a few more pearls to cast."

PELICAN

A man walked into a doctor's office with a pelican on his head.

"You need help immediately," said the doctor.

"I certainly do," said the pelican. "Get this man out from under me."

PENNIES

One reason we have so many pennies in the church collection plate is because we have no smaller coin.

PENNY SCALE

A penny scale dispensed the following fortune card to a fat lady: "You are very fond of food. You lack willpower and you overdo everything. Either that, or a baby elephant has just collapsed on this scale."

PENNY-PINCHER

A Scotchman was arguing with a conductor as to whether the fare was 25 or 50 cents. Finally the disgusted conductor picked up the Scotchman's suitcase and tossed it off the train, just as they passed over a bridge. The suitcase landed with a splash.

"Mon," screamed the Scotchman, "isn't it enough to try to overcharge me, but now you try to drown my little boy!"

PERFECT AGE

My children are at the perfect age...too old to cry at night and too young to borrow my car.

PERFUME

Anyone who thinks chemical warfare is

something new doesn't know much about women's perfume.

PERSONAL CHECK

An old miser, because of his exceptional thrift, had no friends. Just before he died he called his doctor, lawyer, and minister together around his bedside. "I have always heard you can't take it with you, but I am going to prove you can," he said. "I have $90,000 in cash under my mattress. It's in three envelopes of $30,000 each. I want each of you to take one envelope now and just before they throw the dirt on me, you throw the envelopes in."

The three attended the funeral, and each threw his envelope into the grave. On the way back from the cemetery, the minister said, "I don't feel exactly right. I'm going to confess: I needed $10,000 badly for a new church we are building, so I took out $10,000 and threw only $20,000 in the grave."

The doctor said, "I, too, must confess: I am building a hospital and took $20,000 and threw in only $10,000."

The lawyer said, "Gentlemen, I'm surprised, shocked, and ashamed of you. I don't see how you could hold out that money. I threw in my personal check for the full amount."

PESSIMIST

A pessimist remembers the lily belongs to the

onion family, an optimist that the onion belongs to the lily family.

PIG

Customer: This food isn't fit for a pig!
Waiter: I'm sorry, Sir, I'll bring you some that is.

PINCH

A man and his little girl were on an overcrowded elevator. Suddenly a lady in front turned around, slapped the man, and left in a huff. The little girl remarked, "I didn't like her either, Daddy. She stepped on my toe, so I pinched her."

*　　*　　*

As the crowded elevator descended, Mrs. Wilson became increasingly furious with her husband, who was delighted to be pressed against a gorgeous blonde.

As the elevator stopped at the main floor, the blonde suddenly whirled, slapped Mr. Wilson, and said, "That will teach you to pinch!"

Bewildered, Mr. Wilson was halfway to the parking lot with his wife when he choked, "I—I—didn't pinch that girl."

"Of course you didn't," said his wife, consolingly. "I did."

PLAY IT BY EAR

A man walking along the road saw an Indian lying with his ear to the ground. He went over and listened. The Indian said, "Large wheels, Ford pickup truck, green color, man driving with large police dog next to him, Colorado license plate and traveling about 75 miles per hour."

The man was astounded. "You mean you can tell all that just by listening with your ear to the ground?" he asked.

"Ear to the ground, nothing," said the Indian. "That truck just ran over me."

PLUMBER

Householder: Well, I see you brought your tools with you.

Plumber: Yeah, I'm getting absentminded every day.

* * *

Waiter: Who put that statue under the sink?
Frances: That's no statue...that's the plumber.

POISE

Q. What is the definition of poise?
A. The ability to keep talking while the other guy takes the check.

POISONED COFFEE

The district attorney was cross-examining the murderess.

"And after you had poisoned the coffee and your husband sat at the breakfast table partaking of the fatal dosage, didn't you feel any qualms? Didn't you feel the slightest pity for him, knowing he was about to die and was wholly unaware of it?"

"Yes, there was a moment when I sort of felt sorry for him."

"When was that?"

"When he asked for the second cup."

POLITICIAN

The politician is my shepherd . . . I am in want;
He maketh me to lie down on park benches,
He leadeth me beside still factories;
He disturbeth my soul.
Yea, though I walk through the valley of the
shadow of depression and recession,
I anticipate no recovery, for he is with me.
He prepareth a reduction in my salary in the
presence of my enemies;
He anointeth my small income with great losses;
My expenses runneth over.
Surely unemployment and poverty shall follow me
all the days of my life,
And I shall dwell in a mortgaged house forever.

POLITICS

The difference between a Republican and a Democrat is: One is *in* and the other is *out*.

* * *

I stepped into the men's room once and found this sign posted over one of those hot-air blowers for drying hands: "Push Button and Listen for a Short Message from the Vice President."

* * *

There's one thing the Democrats and Republicans share in common—our money.

* * *

Governmental machinery is the marvelous device which enables ten men to do the work of one.

* * *

A lobbyist browsing through an encyclopedia the other day came upon a stunning idea. In ancient Greece, in order to prevent idiot statesmen from passing stupid laws upon the people, at one point in Greek history lawmakers were asked to introduce all new laws while standing on a platform with a rope around their neck. If the law passed, the rope was removed. If it failed, the platform was removed.

POLYGAMY

A Mormon acquaintance once pushed Mark Twain into an argument on the issue of polygamy. After long and tedious expositions justifying the practice, the Mormon demanded that Twain cite any passage of Scripture expressly forbidding polygamy.

"Nothing easier," Twain replied. "No man can serve two masters."

PONTIUS THE PILOT

A Sunday school teacher asked her students to draw a picture of the Holy Family. After the pictures were brought to her, she saw that some of the youngsters had drawn the conventional pictures—the Holy Family and the manger, the Holy Family riding on the mule, etc.

But she called up one little boy to ask him to explain his drawing, which showed an airplane with four heads sticking out of the plane windows.

She said, "I can understand that you drew three of the heads to show Joseph, Mary, and Jesus. But who's the fourth head?"

"Oh," answered the boy, "that's Pontius the pilot!"

POOR

There's one advantage in being poor...it's very inexpensive.

* * *

"How do you know your family was poor?"
"Every time I passed someone in town, they would say, 'There goes Joe. His poor family!'"

POOR EXCUSE

Jones came into the office an hour late for the third time in one week and found the boss waiting for him. "What's the story this time, Jones?" he asked sarcastically. "Let's hear a good excuse for a change."

Jones sighed, "Everything went wrong this morning, Boss. The wife decided to drive me to the station. She got ready in ten minutes, but then the drawbridge got stuck. Rather than let you down, I swam across the river (look, my suit's still damp), ran out to the airport, got a ride on Mr. Thompson's helicopter, landed on top of Radio City Music Hall, and was carried here piggyback by one of the Rockettes."

"You'll have to do better than that, Jones," said the boss, obviously disappointed. "No woman can get ready in ten minutes."

POPEYE

A man sought medical aid because he had popped eyes and a ringing in his ears. A doctor looked him over and suggested removal of his tonsils. The operation resulted in no improvement, so the patient consulted another doctor, who suggested removal of his teeth. The teeth were extracted, but still the man's eyes popped and the ringing in his ears continued.

A third doctor told him bluntly, "You've got six months to live." In that event, the doomed man decided he would treat himself right while he could. He bought a flashy car, a chauffeur, and the best tailor in town to make him 30 suits, and decided even his shirts would be made-to-order.

"Okay," said the shirtmaker, "let's get your measurements. Hmm, 35 sleeve, 16 collar—"

"Fifteen," the man said.

"Sixteen collar," the shirtmaker repeated, measuring again.

"But I've always worn a 15 collar," said the man.

"Listen," the shirtmaker said, "I'm warning you. You keep on wearing a 15 collar, and your eyes will pop and you'll have a ringing in your ears."

PORSCHE

A woman offered a brand-new Porsche for sale for a price of ten dollars. A man answered the ad, but he was slightly disbelieving.

"What's the gimmick?" he inquired.

"No gimmick," the woman answered. "My husband died, and in his will he asked that the car be sold and the money go to his secretary."

PRAISE THE LORD

Did you hear about the country parson who decided to buy himself a horse? The dealer assured him that the one he selected was a perfect choice. "This here horse," he said, "has lived all his life in a religious atmosphere. So remember that he'll never start if you order 'Giddyap.' You've got to say, 'Praise the Lord.' Likewise, a 'Whoa' will never make him stop. You've got to say, 'Amen.'"

Thus forewarned, the parson paid for the horse, mounted him, and with a cheery "Praise the Lord" sent him wandering off in the direction of the parson's parish. Suddenly, however, he noticed that the road ahead had been washed out, leaving a chasm 200 yards deep. In a panic, he forgot his instructions and cried "Whoa" in vain several times. The horse just cantered on. At the very last moment he remembered to cry "Amen"...and the horse stopped short at the very brink of the chasm. But alas! That's when the parson, out of force of habit, murmured fervently, "Praise the Lord!"

PRAYER

A farmer was in town at noon and went into a

restaurant for a hamburger and french fries. When he was served, he quietly bowed his head and gave the Lord thanks for his food.

Some rough-looking fellows at the next table saw him and thought they would give him a hard time. One of them called out, "Hey, Farmer, does everyone do that where you live?"

"No, Son," answered the farmer, "the pigs and donkeys don't."

PREACHING

One Sunday a farmer went to church. When he entered he saw that he and the preacher were the only ones present. The preacher asked the farmer if he wanted him to go ahead and preach. The farmer said, "I'm not too smart, but if I went to feed my cattle and only one showed up, I'd feed him." So the minister began his sermon.

One hour passed, then two hours, then two-and-a-half hours. The preacher finally finished and came down to ask the farmer how he had liked the sermon.

The farmer answered slowly, "Well, I'm not very smart, but if I went to feed my cattle and only one showed up, I sure wouldn't feed him all the hay."

PREDICTION

"If you're such a good fortune-teller, you should be able to tell me the score of tonight's hockey game before it starts!"

"Before the game starts, the score will be nothing to nothing!"

PRESCRIPTION

Did you hear about the doctor who wrote out a prescription in the usual doctor's fashion? The patient used it for two years as a railroad pass. Twice it got him into Radio City Music Hall, and once into Yankee Stadium. It came in handy as a letter from his employer to the cashier to increase his salary. And as a climax, his daughter played it on the piano and won a scholarship to the Curtis Music Conservatory.

PRESIDENT

Father: Son, do you realize when Lincoln was your age he was already studying hard to be a lawyer?

Son: Right, Pop, and when he was your age, he was already President of the United States!

PRIZE

"The man who married my mother got a prize."
"What was it?"

PRODIGAL

A Sunday school class was being quizzed on the

prodigal son. The teacher asked one youngster, "Who was sorry when the prodigal son returned home?"

The boy gave it a lot of deep thought, then said, "The fatted calf."

PROSPERITY

Few of us can stand prosperity—another man's, I mean.

PROTECTION

Son: Why is a man not allowed to have more than one wife?

Father: Because the law protects those who are incapable of protecting themselves.

PSYCHOTICS

Neurotics build air castles. Psychotics live in them. Psychiatrists collect the rent.

PUCKER UP, PARTNER

A little prospector wearing clean new shoes walked into a saloon. A big Texan said to his friend standing at the bar, "Watch me make this dude dance." He walked over to the prospector and said, "You're a foreigner, aren't you? From the East?"

"You might say that," the little prospector answered. "I'm from Boston and I'm here prospecting for gold."

"Now tell me something. Can you dance?"

"No, Sir. I never did learn to dance."

"Well, I'm going to teach you. You'll be surprised how quickly you can learn."

With that, the Texan took out his gun and started shooting at the prospector's feet. Hopping, skipping, jumping, by the time the little prospector made it to the door he was shaking like a leaf.

About an hour later the Texan left the saloon. As soon as he stepped outside the door, he heard a click. He look around and there, four feet from his head, was the biggest shotgun he had ever seen.

The little prospector said, "Mr. Texan, have you ever kissed a mule?"

"No," said the quick-thinking Texan, "but I've always wanted to."

PUMPKIN PIE

When we first married, my wife was not a very good cook. She would make new desserts and have me try them before dinner.

One day I came home and she told me that she had just made a pumpkin pie. She told me to try some. I said, "How about after dinner?"

She said, "No, I want you to try it now."

I don't want to say it was bad, but I had to drink four glassfuls!

PUN

A form of humor that causes everyone to groan and is meant to punish the hearers

PUNISH

Woman: One of your bees just stung me. I want you to do something about it.

Beekeeper: Certainly, Madam. Just show me which bee it was and I'll have it punished.

PURSUED

Deacon: It says here, "The wicked flee when no man pursueth."

Pastor: Yes, that is true, but they make much better time when somebody is after them.

PUSH

Mother: Did you push your little sister down the stairs?

Bobby: I only pushed her down one step. She fell the rest of the way.

* * *

A Baptist minister rushed down to the train station every single day to watch the Sunset Limited go by. There was no chore he wouldn't interrupt to carry out his ritual. Members of his congregation deemed his eccentricity juvenile and frivolous, and asked him to give it up. "No, Gentlemen," he said firmly. "I preach your sermons, teach your Sunday school, bury your dead, marry you, run your charities, chair every drive it pleases you to conduct. I won't give up seeing that Southern Pacific train every day. I love it! It's the only thing in this town I don't have to push!"

QUAKER FEELING HIS OATS

A burglar entered the house of a Quaker and proceeded to rob it. The Quaker heard noises and took his shotgun downstairs and found the burglar. He aimed his gun and said gently: "Friend, I mean thee no harm, but thou standest where I am about to shoot."

QUICK THINKING

A Scotsman and an Englishman were leaning against the counter in a store when a bandit walked in and brandished his gun.

The Scot, a quick thinker, hauled out his money and handed it to his English friend.

He said, "Here's the ten dollars you lent me."

QUICK TOUCH

A village blacksmith working at his open forge, hammering a white-hot horseshoe, had just finished the shoe and thrown it to the ground to cool.

The local wise guy walked in at that moment. He picked up the horseshoe, but dropped it with a howl of pain.

"Pretty hot, eh?" asked the blacksmith.

"Naw," said the wise guy. "It just don't take me long to look over a horseshoe."

RAIN CHECKS

A visitor to a drought-stricken area was engaged in conversation at the local store about the "no-rain" situation.

"You think the drought is bad here," the merchant observed, "but down south o' here a-ways, they haven't had any for so long that the Baptists are sprinkling, the Methodists are using a damp cloth, and the Presbyterians are issuing rain checks!"

RAISE

Employee: I have been here 11 years doing three men's work for one man's pay. Now I want a raise.

Boss: Well, I can't give you a raise, but if you'll tell me who the other two men are, I'll fire them.

RALPH

Myles: Suppose you loan Ralph ten dollars and he agrees to repay you at the rate of a dollar a week. How much money would you have after seven weeks?

Jay: Nothing.

Myles: Nothing? You don't know very much about math.

Jay: You don't know much about Ralph.

RARE BOOK

A collector of rare books ran into an acquaintance of his who had just thrown away an old Bible that had been in his family for generations. He happened to mention that Guten something had printed it.

"Not Gutenberg?" gasped the book collector.

"Yes, that was the name."

"You idiot! You've thrown away one of the first books ever printed. A copy recently sold at an auction for $400,000."

"Mine wouldn't have been worth a dime," replied the man. "Some clown by the name of Martin Luther had scribbled all over it."

RASH

A lady with a bad rash visited a dermatologist. It was the type of condition that had been present for some time.

"Have you been treated for this rash before?" inquired the doctor.

"Yes, by my druggist."

"And what sort of foolish advice did he give you?" asked the doctor.

"Oh, he told me to come and see you."

RAZOR

Jim: I got one of those new razors that has twin blades.

Tom: How do you like it?

Jim: Shaves good. But now instead of getting nicks, I get ditto marks.

REAL SAFE

Wife: You know the old saying, "What you don't know won't hurt you"?

Husband: What about it?

Wife: You must really be safe.

A REAL TRIP

A man was walking down some stairs when all of a sudden he slipped. In the process a stout lady toppled against him and they ended up on the bottom step with the lady sitting in the man's lap. The man tapped the lady on the shoulder. "I'm sorry, Lady," he rasped, "but this is as far as I go."

A REAL TURN-ON

Did you hear about the Indian chief named Running Water? He had two daughters—Hot and Cold—and a son named Luke.

REALITY

A mother, visiting a department store, took her son to the toy department. Spying a gigantic rocking horse the boy climbed up on it and rocked back and forth for almost an hour.

"Come on, Son," the mother pleaded. "I have to get home to get father's dinner."

The little lad refused to budge, and all her efforts were unavailing. The department manager also tried to coax the little fellow without meeting with any success. Eventually, in desperation they called the store's psychiatrist. Gently he walked over and whispered a few words in the boy's ear, and immediately the lad jumped off and ran to his mother's side.

"How did you do it?" the mother asked incredibly. "What did you say to him?"

The psychiatrist hesitated for a moment, then said, "All I said was, 'If you don't jump off that rocking horse at once, son, I'll knock the stuffing out of you!' "

RECEPTION COMMITTEE

About three weeks before an annual club dinner, a member received a letter from the club president, asking him to serve on the reception committee and be there at seven o'clock sharp. A scarlet ribbon marked RECEPTION COMMITTEE was enclosed. He hadn't meant to go. The dinners were usually a bore. But since he had been asked to be on the committee, he decided to go.

By the time he arrived, almost all 800 members of the club were there, each wearing a scarlet ribbon marked RECEPTION COMMITTEE.

REDUCING

The worst kind of reducing pill is the one who keeps telling you how he did it.

* * *

"My wife has been using a flesh-reducing roller for nearly two months."

"And can you see any result yet?"

"Yes—the roller is much thinner."

REFRIGERATOR

A woman went to her psychiatrist and said, "Doctor, I want to talk to you about my husband. He thinks he's a refrigerator."

"That's not so bad," said the doctor. "It's a rather harmless complex."

"Well, maybe," replied the lady. "But he sleeps with his mouth open and the light keeps me awake."

RELAXATION

Advice to mothers: Unless you deliberately set

aside a little time for regular relaxation, you will
not be able to efficiently care for your family.
Therefore, plan to relax a minimum of an hour and
a half every 15 years.

REMEMBER

A worker was called on the carpet by his
supervisor for talking back to his foreman. "Is it
true that you called him a liar?"

"Yes, I did."

"Did you call him stupid?"

"Yes."

"Slave driver?"

"Yes."

"And did you call him an opinionated,
bullheaded egomaniac?"

"No, but would you write that down so I can
remember it?"

REPETITION

Boss: The main thing to remember is that
repetition, repetition, repetition is the keynote! If
you have a product to sell, keep harping on it every
possible way, cram it down people's throats...make
yourself sickening and repulsive if you have to, but
don't ever forget to repeat and repeat and repeat!
It's the only way to get results!

Employee: Yes, Sir.

Boss: And now, what was it you came in to see me about?

Employee: Well, Sir, a raise! A raise! A raise! A raise! A raise! A raise! A raise! A raise...

REPORT CARD

Here's my report card...and I'm tired of watching TV anyway.

RESTLESS

After a great host of boring speakers had spoken, the last speaker rose to the platform clutching a bulky prepared speech. The guests could hardly conceal their restlessness. However, he made many friends when he said, "Friends, it's so late I've decided to just mail each of you a copy of this speech." Then he bowed and sat down.

RETAIL STORE

Q. If a dog lost his tail, where would he get another one?

A. At the retail store, naturally.

REVENUE

Internal Revenue man, eyeing taxpayer's expense claims: "Shall we go over this item by item, or would you prefer to chicken out right now?"

REVERSE REASON

She married him because he was such a "dominating man"; she divorced him because he was such a "dominating male."

He married her because she was so "fragile and petite"; he divorced her because she was so "weak and helpless."

She married him because "he knows how to provide a good living"; she divorced him because "all he thinks about is business."

He married her because "she reminds me of my mother"; he divorced her because "she's getting more like her mother every day."

She married him because he was "happy and romantic"; she divorced him because he was "shiftless and fun-loving."

He married her because she was "steady and sensible"; he divorced her because she was "boring and dull."

She married him because he was "the life of the party"; she divorced him because "he never wants to come home from a party."

RICH

Beverly: A scientist says that what we eat we become.

Melba: Oh, boy! Let's order something rich.

RICH RELATIVE

Q. What type of person lives the longest?
A. A rich relative.

THE RIGHT ROW

A man and his wife were running to their seats after a movie intermission. In a voice of concern, he asked a man at the end of a row, "Did I step on your toes on the way out?"

"You certainly did," responded the other angrily.

"All right," he said, turning to his wife. "This is our row."

RIP VAN WINKLE

A modern-day Rip Van Winkle slept for 20 years. Upon awaking he immediately called his broker.

"What's the stock market done the past 20 years?" he inquired.

With the aid of a computer, his broker soon was able to report that his 100 shares of AT&T were now worth $9.5 million, his 100 shares of General Motors worth $7.9 million, and his oil holdings had increased to $19 million.

"Great!" Rip exclaimed. "I'm rich!"

At which point the telephone operator interrupted and said, "Your three minutes are up, Sir. Would you please deposit a million dollars?"

ROAD MAPS

First husband: I think my wife is getting tired of me.

Second husband: What makes you feel that way?

First husband: She keeps wrapping my lunches in road maps.

ROBBED

The teller had just been robbed for the third time by the same man, and the police officer was asking if he had noticed anything specific about the criminal.

"Yes," said the teller, "he seems to be better dressed each time."

ROCK 'N' ROLL

Advertisement in newspaper: For sale cheap...my son's collection of rock 'n' roll records. If a boy's voice answers the phone, hang up and call later.

RUDOLPH THE RED

Mr. and Mrs. Smith were touring Russia. Their guide argued all the time. As the couple was leaving Moscow, the husband said, "Look, it's snowing out."

The guide disagreed, "No, Sir, it's raining out."

I still think it's snowing," said Mr. Smith.

But his wife replied, "Rudolph the Red knows rain, Dear."

RULE THE WORLD

Husband: I know you are having a lot of trouble with the baby, Dear, but keep in mind, "the hand that rocks the cradle is the hand that rules the world."

Wife: How about taking over the world for a few hours while I go shopping?

RUMBLE, RUMBLE

An Army base staff that was planning war games did not want to use live ammunition. Instead they informed the men: "In place of a rifle, you go 'Bang, bang.' In place of a knife, you go 'Stab, stab.' In place of a hand grenade, you go 'Lob, lob ' "

The game was in progress when one of the soldiers saw one of the enemy. He went "Bang, bang,' but nothing happened. He ran forward and went "Stab, stab," but nothing happened. He ran back and went "Lob, lob," but nothing happened. Finally he walked up to the enemy and said, "You are not playing fair. I went 'Bang, bang,' and 'Stab, stab,' and, 'Lob, lob,' and you haven't fallen dead yet!"

The enemy responded, "Rumble, rumble. I'm a tank."

RUMOR

A flying rumor never has any trouble in making a landing.

RUSSIAN

This big-wheel Russian is riding along when he sees a peasant kneeling in the middle of a field, praying. He stops the car, stomps over, and says, "Aha! You waste your time like this instead of plowing and planting for the Party!"

"But Commissar, I'm praying for the Party!"

"Praying for the Party! Huh! And years ago, you probably prayed for the Czar!"

"I did, Commissar."

"Well...look what happened to him!"

"Right."

ST. PETER

An exasperated mother, whose son was always getting into mischief, finally asked him, "How do you expect to get into heaven?"

The boy thought it over and said, "Well, I'll just run in and out and in and out and keep slamming the door until St. Peter says, 'For heaven's sake, Jimmy, come in or stay out.' "

SALES, NOT MANAGEMENT

An airliner flew into a violent thunderstorm and

was soon swaying and bumping around the sky. One very nervous lady happened to be sitting next to a clergyman and turned to him for comfort. "Can't you do something?" she demanded forcefully.

"I'm sorry, Ma'am," said the reverend gently. "I'm in sales, not management."

SALESMAN

A man walked into a men's clothing store and told the manager he wanted a job as a salesman.

"Sorry, we don't need any salesmen," the manager told him.

"But you've just got to hire me," the man said. "I'm the world's greatest salesman!"

The sales manager again refused, but the man hung on and was so convincing that finally the manager said, "Okay, I'll tell you what I'll do. See that suit over there hanging on the back wall? After you've dusted it off, you'll see that it has padded shoulders, pointed lapels, and a belt in the back. It's sort of a blue-orange-green-purple plaid. I don't even remember how I got stuck with it. Now, I'm going to lunch and I'm going to leave you in charge. If you can sell that suit before I get back, you're hired."

About an hour later the manager returned to find the store in a mess. The rugs were ripped, a showcase was turned over, and merchandise was all over the floor, but the suit was gone.

"Well, I see you've sold the suit."

"Yes, Sir."

"It looks like you had a little trouble with the customer, though."

"No, Sir. Not a bit of trouble with the customer—but oh, that seeing-eye dog."

SANDWICH

Customer: Waiter, will you bring me another sandwich, please?

Waiter: Will there be anything else?

Customer: Yes, a paperweight. My first sandwich blew away.

SANTA CLAUS

The three stages of man: He believes in Santa Claus; he does not believe in Santa Claus; he is Santa Claus.

SATISFACTION

A man sitting at his window one evening casually called to his wife, "There goes that woman Ken Roberts is in love with."

His wife in the kitchen dropped the plate she was drying, ran into the living room, knocked over a vase, and looked out the window.

"Where, where?" she asked.

"Over there," said the husband. "The woman in the blue dress standing on the corner."

"Why, you big idiot," she replied, "that's his wife."

"Yes, of course," answered the husband with a satisfied grin.

SAWMILL

Ken: I slept like a log.
Melba: Yes, I heard the sawmill.

SAY IT AGAIN

I would like to present the funniest, most talented, most outstanding speaker and the fellow who wrote this introduction for me...

SCAFFOLDING

Ken: My uncle fell off a scaffolding and was killed.
Bob: What was he doing up on the scaffolding?
Ken: Getting hanged.

SCHOOL DAYS

School days are the best days of your life... provided your children are old enough to go.

SCHOOLTEACHER

A wise schoolteacher sends this note to all parents on the first day of school: "If you promise not to believe everything your child says happens at school, I'll promise not to believe everything he says happens at home."

SEASON TICKET

First man: My wife just got a ticket for speeding.
Second man: That's nothing! My wife is so bad the police gave her a season ticket.

SEND THE BILL

Doctor: I can do nothing for your sickness. It is hereditary.
Patient: Then send the bill to my father.

SENIOR

You can tell a freshman,
  by his slaphappy look.
You can tell a sophomore,
  because he carries a comic book.
You can tell a junior,
  by his debonairness and such.
You can tell a senior,
  but you can't tell him much.

SENSE

Son: Do you think a man has more sense after he is married?

Father: Yes, but it's too late then.

SERMON

Rocking horse sermon—back and forth, back and forth, but going nowhere.

Mockingbird sermon—repetition, nothing new.

Smorgasbord sermon—a little bit of everything, but nothing solid.

Jericho sermon—march around the subject seven times.

Christmas tree sermon—something offered for nothing.

*   *   *

One beautiful Sunday morning, a minister announced to his congregation: "My good people, I have here in my hands three sermons—a $100 sermon that lasts five minutes, a $50 sermon that lasts fifteen minutes and a $10 sermon that lasts a full hour. Now, we'll take the collection and see which one I'll deliver."

*   *   *

Visitor: How long has your minister been preaching?

Member: About 30 years.

Visitor: He ought to be through soon.

SERVES YOU RIGHT

Boy: Dad, Mom just backed the car out of the garage and ran over my bicycle.

Father: Serves you right, Son, for leaving it on the front lawn.

SERVICE

A man who had been married for ten years was consulting a marriage counselor. "When I was first married, I was very happy. I'd come home from a hard day down at the shop, and my little dog would race around barking, and my wife would bring my slippers. Now everything's changed. When I come home, my dog brings my slippers, and my wife barks at me."

"I don't know what you're complaining about," said the counselor. "You're still getting the same service."

SHAMPOO

"What happened to the other barber that used to be here?"

"Well, he is now in the home for the insane. One day, when his business was slow, he asked a customer if he wanted a shampoo and the customer said 'No.' I guess that was the last straw. He took a razor and slashed the customer's throat. By the way, how about a shampoo today?"

"Sure, go ahead," said the customer.

THE SHIRT OFF YOUR BACK

The story is told of a corporal who reported to a new regiment with a letter from his old captain, saying, "This man is a great soldier, and he'll be even better if you can cure him of his constant gambling."

The new commanding officer looked at him sternly and said, "I hear you're an inveterate gambler. I don't approve. It's bad for discipline. What kind of thing do you bet on?"

"Practically anything, Sir," said the corporal. "If you'd like, I'll bet you my next month's pay that you've got a strawberry birthmark under your right arm."

The C.O. snapped, "Put down your money." He then stripped to the waist, proved conclusively he had no birthmark, and pocketed the bills on the table. He couldn't wait to phone the captain and exult, "That corporal of yours won't be in a hurry to make a bet after what I just did to him."

"Don't be too sure," said the captain mournfully. "He just wagered me 20 to 200 he'd get you to take your shirt off five minutes after he reported."

SHOE REPAIR

While rummaging through his attic, a man found a shoe-repair ticket that was nine years old. Figuring that he had nothing to lose, he went to the shop and presented the ticket to the proprietor, who reluctantly began a search for the unclaimed shoes. After ten minutes, the owner reappeared and handed back the ticket.

"Well," asked the customer, "did you find the pair?"

"Yes," replied the shop owner. "They'll be ready Tuesday."

SHOT

"I shot my dog."

"Was he mad?"

"Well, it didn't seem to exactly please him."

SHOWER

An old philosopher of Greece once received a severe tongue-lashing from his wife. When he listened in silence, she was the more infuriated; so she picked up a pail of cold water and threw it over him, drenching him from head to foot.

With the water still dripping from him, very calmly he remarked, "After that thunder and lightning, I rather expected a shower."

SICK SACK

My airplane flight was so rough that the

stewardesses poured the food directly into the sick sacks!

SIDE

Sir, my concern is not whether God is on our side; my great concern is to be on God's side, for God is always right.

SIGN

Sign outside house in the city:

TRESPASSERS WILL BE PROSECUTED TO THE FULL EXTENT OF ONE GERMAN SHEPHERD.

*   *   *

Outside a house in Sussex, England: "Beware of owner. Never mind the dog."

*   *   *

Sign on garbage truck:

SATISFACTION GUARANTEED, OR DOUBLE YOUR GARBAGE BACK.

*   *   *

"What sign were you born under?"
"Quiet—Hospital Zone."

SILENCE

Father: Did Paul bring you home last night?

Daughter: Yes, it was late, Daddy. Did the noise disturb you?

Father: No, My Dear, it wasn't the noise. It was the silence.

SIN

A nice but blundering old lady liked the new pastor and wanted to compliment him as she was leaving church after services. So she said to him, "I must say, Sir, that we folks didn't know what sin was until you took charge of our parish."

SLAPPED

The story is told of a young Czechoslovakian, a Russian officer, a little old lady, and an attractive young woman riding on a train.

Shortly after the train entered a dark tunnel, the passengers heard a kiss, then a loud slap.

The young woman thought: "Isn't that odd the Russian tried to kiss the old lady and not me?"

The old lady thought: "That is a good girl with fine morals."

The Russian officer thought: "That Czech is a smart fellow; he steals a kiss and I get slapped."

The Czech thought: "Perfect. I kiss the back of my hand, clout a Russian officer, and get away with it."

SLIDE OVER

Wife: Before we were married, we didn't sit this far apart in the car.

Husband: Well, Dear, I didn't move.

SLOW

"Look here, Private, this man beside you on this fatigue detail is doing twice the work you are."

"I know, Sarge. That's what I've been telling him for the last hour, but he won't slow down."

SLOWLY

Mr. and Mrs. McKee, vacationing in Rome, were being shown through the Colosseum.

"Now, this room," said the guide, "is where the slaves dressed to fight the lions."

"But how does one dress to fight lions?" inquired Mr. McKee.

"Very slow-w-w-w-w-wly," replied the guide.

*　　*　　*

George was having trouble with a toothache, so he decided to visit the dentist.

"What do you charge for extracting a tooth?" George asked.

"Five dollars," replied the dentist.

"Five dollars for only two minutes' work?" exclaimed George.

"Well," replied the dentist, "if you wish, I can extract it very slowly."

SMALL HUMOR

Q. How do you milk an ant?
A. First, you get a low stool...

SMART

Blow: Did you hear the smartest kid in the world is becoming deaf?
Joe: No, tell me about it.
Blow: What did you say?

SMART TALK

"You're not smart enough to talk to an idiot!"
"Okay! I'll send you a letter!"

SMILE

To make a smile come, so they say,
   brings 15 muscles into play.
But if you want a frown to thrive
   you have to use some 65!

* * *

"Did you see that young lady smile at me?"
"That's nothing. The first time I saw you, I laughed right out loud. '

SMOKE

Jay: Does the Bible say that if you smoke you can't get to heaven?

Bufe: No, but the more you smoke the quicker you'll get there.

SMOKING

Did you hear about the man who read that smoking was bad for your health? He immediately gave up reading.

SNAKE

Did you hear the story about the fisherman who was fishing with the only thing the fish would bite on—frogs? In searching for frogs, which were rather scarce, he saw a big garden snake with a frog in its mouth, but the snake would not release it. He did not know what to do. As he looked around, he noticed an old whiskey bottle on the shore that someone had tossed aside and it still had some whiskey in it. He grabbed the bottle and poured the leftover whiskey on the snake's head. The snake finally coughed up the frog.

The fisherman baited his hook with the frog and went back to fishing. Everything was going well until he felt something crawling up his pant leg. He looked down and there was the same snake with another frog in its mouth.

SNORING

Why is it that the loudest snorer is always the first one to get to sleep?

SO YOU THINK YOU HAVE TROUBLES!

When I got to the building, I found that the hurricane had knocked some bricks off the top. So I rigged up a beam with a pulley at the top of the building and hoisted up a couple of barrels full of bricks. When I had fixed the building, there were a lot of bricks left over. Then I went to the bottom of the building and cast off the line. Unfortunately, the barrel of bricks was heavier than I was, and before I knew what was happening, the barrel started down, jerking me off the ground.

I decided to hang on and halfway up I met the barrel coming down and received a hard blow on the shoulder. I then continued to the top, banging my head against the beam and getting my fingers jammed in the pulley. When the barrel hit the ground, it burst its bottom, allowing all the bricks to spill out.

I was now heavier than the barrel and so started down again at high speed. Halfway down I met the barrel coming up and received more injuries to my shins.

When I hit the ground, I landed on the bricks, getting several painful cuts. At this point I must have lost my presence of mind because I let go the line. The barrel came down, giving me another heavy blow on the head and putting me in the hospital.

I respectfully request sick leave.

SOFT MUSIC

Some people ask the secret of our long marriage. We take time to go to a restaurant two times a week: a little candlelight dinner, soft music, and a slow walk home. She goes Tuesdays; I go Fridays.

SOME CAN—SOME CAN'T

The inmates of a prison had a joke book they all had memorized. The way they recited the jokes was by the number of the joke. Some fellow would call out a number from one to one hundred and all would laugh.

A new man in the prison, after studying the book, said he wanted to tell a joke. They said, "Okay, shoot!"

He said, "Number 20," but nobody laughed. He said, "This is funny. What's wrong; why aren't you laughing?"

A fellow nearby said, "Some can tell them and some can't."

SOME GO

Some go to church to weep, while others go to sleep.

Some go to tell their woes, others to show their clothes.

Some go to hear the preacher, others like the solo screecher.

Boys go to reconnoiter, girls go because they orter.

Many go for good reflections, precious few to help collections.

SON

One employee to another employee: "When the boss' son starts working here tomorrow, he'll have no special privileges or authority. Treat him just as you would anyone else who was due to take over the whole business in a year or two."

SON-IN-LAW

"Was that your wife I saw you with last night?"

"No, that was my son-in-law, and I could cry every time I think about it."

SPEECH

Upon entering a room in a hotel, a woman recognized a well-known government official pacing up and down and asked what he was doing there. "I am going to deliver a speech," he said.

"Do you usually get very nervous before addressing a large audience?"

"Nervous?" he replied. "No, I never get nervous."

"In that case," demanded the lady, "what are you doing in the ladies room?"

*   *   *

Delivering a speech at a banquet on the night of his arrival in a large city, a visiting minister told several anecdotes he expected to repeat at meetings the next day. Because he wanted to use the jokes again, he requested the reporters to omit them from any accounts they might turn in to their newspapers. A cub reporter, in commenting on the speech, ended his piece with the following: "The minister told a number of stories that cannot be published."

SPHINX

Professor: Jones, can you tell me who built the Sphinx?

Student: I-I-I did know, Sir, but I've forgotten!

Professor: Great guns, what a calamity! The only man living who knows, and he has forgotten!

SPIT ON YOU

I don't smoke but I chew. Don't blow your smoke on me, and I won't spit on you.

SPLINTER

Bill: I've got a splinter in my finger.
Jill: How did you get it...scratch your head?

*　　*　　*

Chet: How did you get your hand full of splinters?
Jack: I was out hunting and caught a timber wolf bare-handed.

SPRINGTIME

On the first day of springtime my true love gave to me: five packs of seed, four sacks of fertilizer, three cans of weed killer, two bottles of insect spray, and a pruning knife for the pear tree.

STATION

A janitor who worked in a railroad station decided to get married in a huge room on the upper floor of the station. So many friends and kinfolk showed up that their combined weight caused the building to collapse.

Moral of the story: Never marry above your station.

STEADY

Bill: I'm a steady worker.

Bob: Yeah, and if you were any steadier, you would be motionless.

STEPPING-STONES

There were three men in a boat halfway across a lake. The first man suddenly said, "I forgot my lunch," got out of the boat, and walked to shore on top of the water.

Later, the second man said, "I forgot my fishing tackle," and also walked across the water to shore.

By this time, the third man thought to himself, "They're not going to outsmart me. I forgot my bait can," and he started to walk across the water, but he sank.

The first man said to the second, "Maybe we should have told him where the rocks were."

STONE

"My husband didn't leave a bit of insurance."

"Then where did you get that gorgeous diamond ring?"

"Well, he left $1,000 for his casket and $5,000 for a stone. This is the stone."

STORK

On his first visit to the zoo, a little boy stared at the caged stork for a long while. Then he turned to his father and exclaimed, "Gee, Dad, he doesn't recognize me."

*　　*　　*

"What do you think of your new little brother, Dear?"

"I wish we'd thrown him away and kept the stork instead."

STORY

We like the fellow who says he is going to make a long story short, and does.

STRAIGHT AND NARROW

The dull thing about going the straight and narrow path is that you so seldom meet anybody you know.

STRAIGHT FACE

Father: When I was your age, I never kissed a girl. Will you be able to tell your children that?

Son: Not with a straight face.

STRIFE

If you want to avoid domestic strife, don't marry in January...and that goes for the other months, too.

STUPID

She: I had to marry you to find out how stupid you are.

He: You should have known that the minute I asked you.

STUPID IDIOT

Two men drove their cars toward each other on a narrow street—neither could pass. One leaned out and shouted, "I never back up for a stupid idiot!"

"I always do!" shouted the other man, shifting into reverse.

SUBJECT

Clara: My pastor is so good he can talk on any subject for an hour.

Sarah: That's nothing! My pastor can talk for an hour without a subject!

SUCCESS

They say success is 90-percent perspiration—you must be a tremendous success!

SUED

Jack and Jill
Went up the hill

To fetch a pail
   Of water.
Jack fell down
   And broke his crown,
And sued the farmer
   And his daughter.

SUGAR

Ben: One of our little pigs was sick so I gave him some sugar.

Dan: Sugar! What for?

Ben: Haven't you ever heard of sugar-cured ham?

SUNDAY SCHOOL

The road to success is dotted with many tempting parking spaces.

*   *   *

Son: Dad, did you go to Sunday school when you were young?

Dad: Never missed a Sunday.

Son: Bet it won't do me any good, either.

SUPPORT

Father: Can you support her in the way she's been accustomed to?

Prospective son-in-law: No, perhaps I can't support her in the manner she has been accustomed to, but I can support her in the way her mother was accustomed to when she first married.

SURE THING

"If you refuse to marry me, I will die," said the young romantic. And, sure enough, 50 years later he died.

SURLY

Cheerful people, the doctors say, resist disease better than the glum ones. In other words, the surly bird catches the germ.

SURPRISE

After an introduction like that, I can hardly wait to hear what I am going to say myself.

SWAP

Seems that a tribal chieftain's daughter was offered as a bride to the son of a neighboring potentate in exchange for two cows and four sheep. The big swap was to be effected on the shore of the stream that separated the two tribes. Pop and his daughter showed up at the appointed time, only to discover that the groom and his livestock were on the other side of the stream. The father grunted, "The fool doesn't know which side his bride is bartered on."

SWING SET

The proud father brought home a backyard swing set for his children and immediately started to assemble it with all the neighborhood children anxiously waiting to play on it. After several hours of reading the directions, attempting to fit bolt A into slot B, etc., he finally gave up and called upon an old handyman working in a neighboring yard.

The old-timer came over, threw the directions away, and in a short while had the set completely assembled.

"It's beyond me," said the father, "how you got it together without even reading the instructions."

"To tell the truth," replied the old-timer, "I can't read, and when you can't read, you've got to think."

THE SYSTEM

Advertising manager: Where did you get this wonderful follow-up system? It would drag money out of anybody.

Assistant: I'll say it would. It's compiled from the letters my son wrote me from college.

TACT

Social tact is making your company feel at home even though you wish they were.

TAILLIGHT

"Pull over to the curb," said the policeman. "You don't have a taillight."

The motorist stepped out, looked in back of the car, and stood quivering and speechless. "Oh, it's not that bad," said the policeman.

The man mumbled, "It's not the taillight I'm worried about. Where is my wife and trailer?"

TAKE IT SLOW

A bachelor kept a cat for companionship, and loved his cat more than life. He was planning a trip to England and entrusted the cat to his brother's care.

As soon as he arrived in England, he called his brother. "How is my cat?" he asked.

"Your cat is dead," came the reply.

"Oh my," he exclaimed. "Did you have to tell me that way?"

"How else can I tell you your cat's dead?" inquired the brother.

"You should have led me up to it gradually," said the bachelor. "For example, when I called tonight you could have told me my cat was on the roof, but the Fire Department is getting it down. When I called tomorrow night, you could have told me they dropped him and broke his back, but a fine surgeon is doing all he can for him. Then, when I called the third night, you could have told me the surgeon did all he could but my cat passed away. That way it wouldn't have been such a shock."

"By the way," he continued, "how's Mother?"

"Mother?" came the reply. "Oh, she's up on the roof, but the Fire Department is getting her down."

TAKE THE BOOKS

The burglars had tied and gagged the bank cashier after extracting the combination to the safe and had herded the other employees into a separate room under guard. After they rifled the safe and were about to leave, the cashier made desperate pleading noises through the gag. Moved by curiosity, one of the burglars loosed the gag.

"Please," whispered the cashier, "take the books, too. I'm $8,500 short."

TAKE TWO ASPIRINS

A doctor had a problem with a leak in his bathroom plumbing that became bigger and bigger. Even though it was 2 A.M., the doctor decided to phone his plumber.

"For Pete's sake, Doc," he wailed, "this is some time to wake a guy."

"Well," the doctor answered testily, "you've never hesitated to call me in the middle of the night with a medical problem. Now it just happens I've got a plumbing emergency."

There was a moment's silence. Then the plumber spoke up, "Right you are, Doc," he agreed. "Tell me what's wrong."

The doctor explained about the leak in the bathroom.

"Tell you what to do," the plumber offered. "Take two aspirins every four hours and drop them down the pipe. If the leak hasn't cleared up by morning, phone me at the office."

TAKE-OUT SERVICE

Passenger: Say, Stewardess, this is the worst steak I ever had. Don't you stewardesses even know how to serve a steak? Bring me another steak right now!

Stewardess: Will that be to take out?

TALK ABOUT NEAT

One thing I'll say for my wife, she's a very neat housekeeper. If I drop my socks on the floor, she picks them up. If I throw my clothes around, she hangs them up. I got up at three o'clock the other morning and went in the kitchen to get a glass of orange juice. I came back and found the bed made.

TALKING

Son: What do you call it when one woman is talking?

Dad: Monologue.

Son: What do you call it when two women are talking?

Dad: Cat-alogue.

*   *   *

The other day I was driving under the influence of my husband. He talks and talks. He gets 2,000 words to the gallon.

TALKING DOG

A man tried to sell his neighbor a new dog.

"This is a talking dog," he said. "And you can have him for five dollars."

The neighbor said, "Who do you think you're kidding with this talking-dog stuff? There ain't no such animal."

Suddenly the dog looked up with tears in his eyes. "Please buy me, Sir," he pleaded. "This man is cruel. He never buys me a meal, never bathes me, never takes me for a walk. And I used to be the richest trick dog in America. I performed before kings. I was in the Army and was decorated ten times."

"Hey!" said the neighbor. "He can talk. Why do you want to sell him for just five dollars?"

"Because," said the seller, "I'm getting tired of all his lies."

TAX COLLECTOR

A man walked into the tax collector's office and sat down and smiled at everyone.

"May I help you?" said the clerk in charge.

"No," said the man. "I just wanted to meet the people I have been working for all these years."

TAXES

April 15 should be called Taxgiving Day.

* * *

I'm gonna put all my money into taxes. They're sure to go up.

* * *

Taxpayer: I always pay my income taxes all at once.

Tax collector: But you are allowed to pay them in quarterly installments.

Taxpayer: I know it, but my heart can't stand it four times a year.

TEA

Three Englishmen stopped at a restaurant for a

spot of tea. The waiter appeared with pad and pencil.

"I'll have a glass of weak tea," ordered the first.

"I'll have tea, too," said the second, "but very strong with two pieces of lemon."

"Tea for me, too, please," said the third. "But be sure the glass is absolutely clean."

In a short time the waiter was back with the order. "All right," he asked "Which one gets the clean glass?"

TEENAGERS

"What did your teenage daughter do all summer?"

"Her hair and her nails!"

*   *   *

Father to teenage son: "Do you mind if I use the car tonight? I'm taking your mother out and I would like to impress her."

*   *   *

Dad: Did you use the car last night?

Son: Yes, Dad. I took some of the boys for a ride.

Dad: Well, tell them I found two of their lipsticks.

*   *   *

Father (to teenage daughter): I want you home by 11 o'clock.

Daughter: But Daddy, I'm no longer a child.

Father: I know, that's why I want you home by 11.

*   *   *

Dialogue between teenager and parent:

"I'm off to the party."

"Well, have a good time."

"Look, Pop, don't tell me what to do."

*   *   *

If you live in a house full of teenagers, it is not necessary to ask for whom the bell tolls. It's not for you.

TEETH

"There will be weeping, wailing, and gnashing of teeth among the wicked who pass on to the next world."

"What about those who haven't got any teeth?"

"Teeth will be provided."

*   *   *

There are three basic rules for having good teeth:

1. Brush them twice a day.

2. See your dentist twice a year.
3. Keep your nose out of other people's business.

TELEVISION

A lot of old TV programs are going off the air and new ones are replacing them, but how can you tell?

TEMPTATION

A driver tucked this note under the windshield wiper of his automobile. "I've circled the block for 20 minutes. I'm late for an appointment, and if I don't park here I'll lose my job. 'Forgive us our trespasses.' "

When he came back he found a parking ticket and this note: "I've circled the block for 20 years, and if I don't give you a ticket, I'll lose my job. 'Lead us not into temptation.' "

TEN POUNDS

"I just lost ten pounds!"
"Turn around; I think I found them!"

TENDER

Q. Why did the locomotive refuse to sit?
A. Because it had a tender behind.

TEXAS

An Easterner was riding with a rancher over a blistering and almost barren stretch of West Texas, when a strange bird scurried in front of them. Asked by the Easterner what the bird was, the rancher replied, "That's a bird of paradise."

The stranger from the East rode on in silence for a moment, then said, "Long way from home, isn't it?"

THAT'S MY SPEECH

Chauncey Depew once played a trick upon Mark Twain on an occasion when they were both to speak at a banquet. Twain spoke first for some 20 minutes and was received with great enthusiasm. When Depew's turn came immediately afterwards, he said, "Mr. Toastmaster, Ladies and Gentlemen, before this dinner Mark Twain and I made an agreement to trade speeches. He has just delivered mine, and I'm grateful for the reception you have accorded it. I regret that I have lost his speech and cannot remember a thing he had to say."

He sat down with much applause.

THAT'S NOTHING

"I caught a 250-pound marlin the other day!"

'That's nothing. I was fishing and hooked a lamp from an old Spanish ship. In fact, the light was still lit!"

"If you will blow out the light, I'll take 200 pounds off the marlin!"

THAT'S ONCE

A couple was celebrating their golden wedding anniversary. Their domestic tranquillity had long been the talk of the town. A local newspaper reporter was inquiring as to the secret of their long and happy marriage.

"Well, it dates back to our honeymoon," explained the lady. "We visited the Grand Canyon and took a trip down to the bottom of the canyon by pack mule. We hadn't gone too far when my husband's mule stumbled. My husband took the mule by the ears, shook him vigorously and said 'That's once.' We proceeded a little farther when the mule stumbled again. Once more my husband took him by the ears, shook him even more vigorously and said, 'That's twice.' We hadn't gone a half-mile when the mule stumbled a third time. My husband promptly removed a revolver from his pocket and shot him. I started to protest over his treatment of the mule when he grabbed me by the ears, shook me vigorously, and said 'That's once.' "

THEOPHILUS

When he was born, the doctor called him "Theophilus." He's theophilus baby I have ever seen.

THEORIES

Before I got married, I had six theories about bringing up children. Now I have six children and no theories.

THIS LITTLE PIGGY WENT TO MARKET

In a small town the farmers of the community had gotten together to discuss some important issues. About midway through the meeting, a wife of one of the farmers stood up and spoke her piece. One old farmer stood up and said, "What does she know about anything? I would like to ask her if she knows how many toes a pig has."

Quick as a flash the woman replied, "Take off your boots, Man, and count them!"

THOUGHTFUL

A tightwad was looking for a gift for a friend. Everything was too expensive except for a glass vase that had been broken and he could purchase it for almost nothing. He asked the store to send it, hoping his friend would think it had been broken in transit.

In due time he received an acknowledgement: "Thanks for the vase," it read. "It was so thoughtful of you to wrap each piece separately."

THREE-HEADED MONSTER

A little boy came home from school crying, "Mommy, Mommy. The kids at school called me a three-headed monster."

The mother responded sympathetically: "Now, there, there, there."

THUNDER

A man went to the psychiatrist because he had a fear of thunder. "Doc, I don't know what to do," said the man.

The doctor replied, "That's ridiculous. Thunder is a natural phenomenon—nothing to be afraid of. Whenever you hear thunder, do like I do: Put your head under the pillow and it will go away."

TIME

A mother of 12 was asked how in the world she could take care of all her children.

"Well," she replied. "When I only had one it took all my time, so how could 11 more make any difference?"

TINY CHUCKLES

Q. What is a small joke called?
A. A mini ha ha.

TITLE

In an age when everyone seems to be playing the name game of glorifying job titles, the man in charge of the meat department at a store in Wichita Falls, Texas, deserves a round of applause. On his weekly time card he describes his position as "Meat Head."

TO HELL AND BACK

Smoking a cigarette won't send you to hell. It just makes you smell like you've been there.

TOENAILS

Joe: What's so unusual about your girlfriend?
Moe: She chews on her nails.
Joe: Lots of girls chew on their nails.
Moe: Toenails?

TOM

"My name is T-t-t-t-tom."
"I'll call you Tom for short."

TOMORROW

Ken: There's nothing like getting up at five in the morning and taking an ice-cold shower and a five-mile jog before breakfast.

Bob: How long have you been doing this?
Ken: I start tomorrow.

* * *

"Remember on our vacation when we spent money like there was no tomorrow? Well, it's tomorrow."

TONGUE

Once when C. H. Spurgeon, then a young man, was passing by the house of a woman with a poison tongue, she let him have a volley of impolite words. "Yes, thank you; I am quite well," Spurgeon said. Then she let out another volley. "Yes, it does look as if it's going to rain," he replied.

Surprised, the woman exclaimed, "Bless the man, he's deaf as a post! What's the use of talking to him?"

TOP THIS

Bill: My dog swallowed a tapeworm and died by inches.

Bob: That's nothing—my dog crawled up in my bed and died by the foot.

Ken: I can beat that. I had a dog that went out of the house and died by the yard.

TRAFFIC FINE

"What am I supposed to do with this?" grumbled the motorist as the police clerk handed him a receipt for his traffic fine.

"Keep it," the clerk advised. "When you get four of them, you get a bicycle."

TRAIN

On a visit to tiny Israel, a Texan boasted: "Why, in Texas you can get on a train, ride for days, and still be in Texas."

His Israeli companion nodded sympathetically. "We have the same trouble with our trains," he said.

TRAIN OF THOUGHT

"Be quiet. You're interrupting my train of thought."

"Let me know when it comes to a station."

TRAIN RIDE

Mark Twain once encountered a friend at the races who said, "I'm broke. I wish you'd buy me a ticket back to town."

Twain said, "Well, I'm pretty broke myself, but I'll tell you what to do. You hide under my seat and I'll cover you with my legs." It was agreed and

Twain then went to the ticket office and bought two tickets. When the train was underway and the supposed stowaway was snug under the seat, the conductor came by and Twain gave him the two tickets.

"Where is the other passenger?" asked the conductor.

Twain tapped on his forehead and said in a loud voice, "That is my friend's ticket. He is a little eccentric and likes to ride under the seat."

TRAIN TO BUFFALO

A big executive boarded a New York-to-Chicago train. He explained to the porter, "I'm a heavy sleeper, and I want you to be sure and wake me at 3:00 A.M. to get off in Buffalo. Regardless of what I say, get me up, for I have some important business there."

The next morning he awakened in Chicago. He found the porter and really poured it on with abusive language.

After he had left, someone said, "How could you stand there and take that kind of talk from that man?"

The porter said, "That ain't nothing. You should nave heard what the man said that I put off in Buffalo."

TRAIN YOUR DOG

A man answered his doorbell and a friend

walked in, followed by a very large dog. As they began talking, the dog knocked over a lamp and jumped up on the sofa with his muddy feet and began chewing on one of the pillows.

The outraged householder, unable to contain himself any longer, burst out, "Don't you think you should train your dog better?"

"*My* dog!" exclaimed the friend, surprised. "I thought it was *your* dog."

TRUCKLOAD OF DUCKS

Teenage daughter (as the radio ground out the final notes of the latest hit song): Did you ever hear anything so wonderful?

Father: Only once—when a truck loaded with empty milk cans bumped another truck filled with live ducks.

TRUMPET

A man mentioned to his landlord about the tenants in the apartment over his. "Many a night they stamp on the floor and shout till midnight."

When the landlord asked if it bothered him, he replied, "Not really, for I usually stay up and practice my trumpet till about that time most every night anyway."

TRUST

One friend said to another, "You drive the car and I'll pray."

"What's the matter—don't you trust my driving?"
"Don't you trust my praying?"

TRYING

Mother, having finally tucked her small boy into bed after an unusually trying day: "Well, I've worked today from son-up to son-down!"

TURKEY

Husband: That is a beautiful turkey for Thanksgiving! What kind of stuffing did you use?

Wife: This one wasn't hollow!

TURNABOUT IS FAIR PLAY

Two girls boarded a crowded bus and one of them whispered to the other, "Watch me embarrass a man into giving me his seat."

Pushing her way through the crowd, she turned all her charms upon a gentleman who looked like he might embarrass easily. "My dear Mr. Wilson," she gushed, "fancy meeting you on the bus. Am I glad to see you. Why, you're almost a stranger. My, but I'm tired."

The sedate gentleman looked up at the girl. He had never seen her before, but he rose and said pleasantly, "Sit down, Mary my girl. It isn't often I see you on washday. No wonder you're tired. Being pregnant isn't easy. By the way, don't deliver the wash until Thursday. My wife is going to the District Attorney's office to see whether she can get your husband out of jail."

TURTLENECK

Tell me, is that your lower lip, or are you wearing a turtleneck sweater?

TWEEDLE

A minister named Tweedle reluctantly refused a Doctor of Divinity degree. He said that he'd rather be Tweedle dumb than Tweedle, D.D.

TWIN

You must be a twin...no one person could be that stupid!

TWINS

Melba: I guess your husband was pleased when he found himself the father of twin boys.
Pam: Was he! He went around grinning from heir to heir.

TWO-CAR GARAGE

Her nostrils are so big that when you kiss her it's like driving into a two-car garage.

UGLY FAT

His wife got rid of 235 pounds of ugly fat...she divorced him.

ULCERS

First wife: Does your husband have ulcers?
Second wife: No, but he's a carrier!

UMPIRES

The devil challenged St. Peter to a baseball game. "How can you win, Satan?" asked St. Peter. "All the famous ballplayers are up here."

"How can I lose?" answered Satan. "All the umpires are down here."

UNBELIEVABLE

A man rose from his seat in a crowded bus so a lady standing nearby could sit down. She was so surprised that she fainted.

When she revived and sat down, she said, "Thanks." Then he fainted.

VACATION

A period of travel and relaxation when you take twice the clothes and half the money you need.

*   *   *

If you can't get away for a vacation, just tip every third person you meet and you'll get the same effect.

VENDING MACHINE

A man put a coin in a vending machine and watched helplessly while the cup failed to appear. One nozzle sent coffee down the drain while another poured cream after it.

"Now that's real automation!" he exclaimed. 'It even drinks for you!"

A VERY SENSITIVE DOG

Did you hear about the dog who played Bach? He was about to be auditioned by a TV producer. The dog's agent warned the producer that this was a very sensitive dog, and that "you had better listen to him play because, if you don't, he loses his temper and leaps at you."

The dog started to play. He was awful. The TV producer patiently waited out the performance. When it was over, he declared angrily, "I should have let him attack. I'm sure his Bach is worse than his bite."

VETERINARIAN

A rancher asked a veterinarian for some free advice. "I have a horse that walks normally sometimes, and sometimes he limps. What shall I do?"

The veterinarian replied, "The next time he walks normally, sell him."

VIC TANNY

A Vic Tanny graduate was boasting about his strength and went on about it for some time. A gardener overheard and made him this offer, "Tell you what. I'll bet you $25 I can wheel a load in this wheelbarrow over there to the other side of the street that you can't wheel back."

"You're on," said Mr. Motormouth. "What's your load going to be?"

"Get in," said the gardener.

VOICE

Pretty young student: Professor Boschovich, do you think I will ever be able to do anything with my voice?

Weary teacher: Well, it might come in handy in case of fire or shipwreck.

*   *   *

The choir had come out of rehearsal.

"Am I to assume that you do a lot of singing at home?" Bill Garrison asked a fellow choir member, Roy Greene.

"Yes, I sing a lot. I use my voice just to kill time," said Roy.

Bill nodded, "You certainly have a fine weapon."

WAITER

Diner: Is it customary to tip the waiter in this restaurant?

Waiter: Why...ah...yes, Sir.

Diner: Then hand me a tip. I've waited almost an hour for that steak I ordered.

WALLET

Did you hear about the fellow that went carp fishing? As he was about to throw his first cast, his wallet fell out of his pocket into the lake. A carp grabbed the wallet and started to swim away with it. Suddenly, another carp ate the carp that had eaten the wallet. Then yet another even larger carp came along and swallowed the carp that ate the carp that devoured the wallet.

An that's how carp-to-carp walleting began.

WATCH THE FIRST STEP

Q. How can you jump off a 50-foot ladder and not get hurt?

A. Jump off the first step.

WE LIKE IT

A fellow had been standing in line to get into a movie theater. He was surprised when he reached the box office because the price for the ticket was $2.50. He pointed to a sign that said "popular prices" and said, "You call $2.50 'popular'?"

"We like it," answered the girl sweetly.

WEAKNESS

Don't judge your wife too harshly for her weaknesses. If she didn't have them, chances are she would never have married you.

WEATHER

Everybody talks about the weather, but nobody does anything about it.

* * *

Don't knock the weather; nine-tenths of the population couldn't start a conversation if the weather didn't change once in a while.

* * *

Probably the last completely accurate weather forecast was when God told Noah there was a 100-percent chance of precipitation.

WEEP AND SNUFFLE

Husband: Why do you weep and snuffle over a TV program and the imaginary woes of people you have never met?

Wife: For the same reason you scream and yell when a man you don't know makes a touchdown.

WEEVILS

Two boll weevils came from the country to the city. One became rich and famous. The other remained the lesser of the two weevils.

WEIGHT

If you really want to lose weight, there are only three things you must give up: breakfast, lunch, and dinner.

WELL-DONE

Husband: "How do you want the electric blanket tonight, Dear...rare, medium or well-done?"

WELL-INFORMED

You can always tell when a man's well-informed. His views are pretty much like your own.

WHALE OF A TAIL

Customer: Your sign says, "Any sandwich you can name." I would like a whale sandwich.

Waiter: Okay. (Disappears into kitchen and shortly returns.) I'm afraid I can't get you a whale sandwich.

Customer: Why not?...your sign says "any sandwich."

Waiter: The cook says he doesn't want to start a new whale for one lousy sandwich.

WHAT A DREAM

Wife: I dreamed you gave me $100 for summer clothes last night. You wouldn't spoil that dream, would you, Dear?

Husband: Of course not, Darling. You may keep the $100.

WHAT A FINNISH

Finn and Huck were friends. Finn up and died. No one was worried, however. They said: "Huck'll bury Finn."

WHAT A MESS

A college boy said to his mother, "I decided that I want to be a political science major and that I want to clean up the mess in the world!"

"That's very nice," purred his mother. "You can go upstairs and start with your room."

WHAT A RELIEF

A man, fond of practical jokes, late one night sent his friend a collect telegram which read: "I am perfectly well."

A week later the joker received a heavy parcel...collect...on which he had to pay considerable charges. On opening it, he found a big block of concrete on which was pasted this message: "This is the weight your telegram lifted from my mind."

WHAT A TAIL

A man was waiting at an intersection for a circus to pass by. He saw a sign on one of the wagons that read: "Barney's Circus with 50 Elephants." He counted the elephants as they crossed the intersection. When he got to 50, he put his car in gear and started to cross the intersection because he was late for an appointment. Unfortunately, he had miscounted and his car hit and killed the last elephant.

A week later he got a notice from the circus that he'd have to pay $200,000. He called the circus manager and inquired, "What's the deal? I only hit one lousy elephant! Why do you want $200,000?"

The manager responded, "It's true, you only hit one elephant, but you pulled the tails out of 49 others!"

WHAT A WRECK

Two truck drivers applied for a job. One said, "I'm Pete and this is my partner, Mike; when I drive at night, he sleeps."

The man said, "All right, I'll give you an oral test. It's three o'clock in the morning. You're on a little bridge and your truck is loaded with nitroglycerin. All of a sudden a truck comes toward you at about 80 miles per hour. What's the first thing you do?"

"I wake up my partner, Mike. He never saw a wreck like this before."

WHAT A YEAR

Melba: My husband was named Man of the Year.
Pam: Well, that shows you what kind of a year it's been.

WHATEVER YOU SAY, DEAR

"Couldn't you get that crook to confess to the crime?" asked the police chief.

"We tried everything, Sir. We browbeat and badgered him with every question we could think of."

"How did he respond?"

"He just dozed off and said now and then: 'Yes, Dear. You are perfectly right.'"

WHAT'S THE BIG DEAL?

Little Billy was left to fix lunch. When his mother returned with a friend, she noticed that Billy had already strained the tea.

"Did you find the tea strainer?" his mother asked.

"No, Mother, I couldn't, so I used the fly swatter," replied Billy.

His mother nearly fainted, so Billy hastily added, "Don't get excited, Mother. I used an old one."

WHERE ARE YOU GOING?

The average man's life consists of 20 years of having his mother ask him where he is going; 40 years of having his wife ask the same question; and at the end, the mourners wonder, too.

WHERE'S MY CAT?

"Hello, police department? I've lost my cat and..."

"Sorry, Sir, that's not a job for the police, we're too busy..."

"But you don't understand...this is a very intelligent cat. He's almost human. He can practically talk."

"Well, you'd better hang up, Sir. He may be trying to phone you right now."

WHERE'S MY PARAKEET?

There's a story going the rounds that involves a carpet layer who had worked all day installing wall-to-wall carpeting. When he noticed a lump under the carpet in the middle of the living room, he felt his shirt pocket for his cigarettes—they were gone. He was not about to take up the carpet, so he went outside for a two-by-four. Stamping down cigarettes with it would be easy. Once the lump was smoothed, the man gathered up his tools and carried them to the truck. Then two things happened simultaneously. He saw his cigarettes on the seat of the truck, and over his shoulder he heard the voice of the woman to whom the carpet belonged. "Have you seen anything of my parakeet?" she asked plaintively.

WHISPER

Boy: Please whisper those three little words that will make me walk on air.

Girl: Go hang yourself.

WHO DO I SHOOT?

A very new soldier was on sentry duty at the main gate of a military outpost. His orders were clear: No car was to enter unless it had a special sticker on the windshield. A big Army car came up with a general seated in the back. The sentry said, "Halt, who goes there?"

The chauffeur, a corporal, said, "General Wheeler."

"I'm sorry, I can't let you through. You've got to have a sticker on the windshield."

The general said, "Drive on."

The sentry said, "Hold it. You really can't come through. I have orders to shoot if you try driving in without a sticker."

The general repeated, "I'm telling you, Son, drive on."

The sentry walked up to the rear window and said, "General, I'm new at this: Do I shoot you or the driver?"

WHO LISTENS?

Two eminently successful psychoanalysts occupied offices in the same building. One was 40 years old, the other over 70. They rode on the elevator together at the end of an unbearably hot, sticky day. The younger man was completely done in, and he noted with some resentment that his senior was fresh as a daisy. "I don't understand," he marveled, "how you can listen to drooling patients from morning till night on a day like this and still look so spry and unbothered when it's over."

The older analyst said simply, "Who listens?"

WHO PAYS THE BILL?

In reply to your request to send a check, I wish to inform you that the present condition of my bank account makes it almost impossible.

My shattered financial conditions are due to federal laws, corporation laws, mothers-in-law, brothers-in-law, sisters-in-law, and outlaws.

Through these taxes I am compelled to pay a business tax, assessment tax, head tax, school tax, income tax, casket tax, food tax, furniture tax, sales tax, and excise tax. Even my brain is taxed.

I am required to get a business license, car license, hunting license, fishing license, truck and auto license, not to mention marriage and dog license. I am also required to contribute to every society and organization which the genius of man is capable of bringing into life; to women's relief, unemployed relief, and gold digger's relief—also to every hospital and charitable institution in the city, including the Red Cross, the Black Cross, the Purple Cross, and the Double Cross.

For my own safety, I am compelled to carry life insurance, liability insurance, burglary insurance, accident insurance, property insurance, business insurance, earthquake insurance, tornado insurance, unemployment insurance, old-age insurance, and fire insurance.

My own business is so governed that it is no easy matter for me to find out who owns it. I am inspected, suspected, disrespected, rejected, dejected, and compelled until I prove an inexhaustible supply of money for every known need of the human race.

Simply because I refuse to donate something or other I am boycotted, talked about, lied about, held up, held down, and robbed until I am almost ruined. I can tell you honestly that except for a miracle that happened I could not enclose this check. The wolf that comes to my door nowadays just had pups in my kitchen. I sold them, and here's the money.

Would like more business to pay more taxes.

Sincerely yours,

WHO'S THAT WOMAN?

Wife: This article on overpopulation of the world says that somewhere in the world there is a woman having a baby every four seconds!

Husband: I think they ought to find that woman and stop her!

WHO'S THERE?

Wife: There is a man at the door who wants to see you about a bill you owe him. He wouldn't give his name.

Husband: What does he look like?

Wife: He looks like you had better pay him.

A WHOLE HOUR

One day an employee arrived late with one eye

closed, his left arm in a sling, and his clothes in tatters. "It's 9:30," pointed out the president, "and you were due at 8:30."

The employee explained, "I fell out of a tenth-story window."

The president snorted and remarked, "It took you a whole hour?"

WILL

A rich uncle died, and a line in his will read as follows: "I leave to my beloved nephew all the money he owes me."

WIND

A tourist traveling through western Kansas saw a man sitting by the ruins of a house that had been blown away.

"Was this your house, My Friend?" he asked sympathetically.

"Yep."

"Any of your family blown away with the house?"

"Yes, wife and four kids."

"Great Scot, Man, why aren't you hunting for them?"

"Well, Stranger, I've been in this country quite a spell. The wind's due to change this afternoon. So I figure I might as well wait here till it brings 'em back."

WINDY

Visitor: Your preacher is sure long-winded.
Member: He may be long...but never winded.

WIPED OUT

The most embarrassing moment in the life of Jane Wyman happened when she was entertaining very special guests. After looking over all the appointments carefully, she put a note on the guest towels, "If you use these, I will murder you." It was meant for her husband. In the excitement she forgot to remove the note. After the guests departed, the towels were discovered still in perfect order, as well as the note itself.

WITS

Bill: I have had to make a living by my wits.
Gill: Well, half a living is better than none.

WITTY

Look, I'm not going to engage in a battle of wits with you. I never attack anyone who's unarmed.

WOLF

A girl can be scared to death by a mouse or a spider, but she's often too willing to take her chances with a wolf.

WOMEN

The way to fight a woman is with your hat. Grab it and run.

WOMEN'S LIB

Did you hear about Glena Zimmerman? She got involved in the women's lib movement and changed her name to Glena Zimmerperson.

*   *   *

A man who traveled to Iran was telling a large audience about how careless the men over there are with their wives. He said it was not an uncommon sight to see a woman and a donkey hitched up together.

From the back of his audience a woman's voice was heard to say, "That's not so unusual. You often see it over here, too."

*   *   *

A girl involved with the women's lib movement boarded a crowded bus and one man rose to his feet.

"No, you must not give up your seat. I insist," she said.

"You may insist as much as you like, Lady," was the reply. "This is my street where I get off."

*   *   *

A women's lib speaker was addressing a large group and said, "Where would man be today if it were not for woman?"

She paused a moment and looked around the room.

"I repeat, where would man be today if it were not for woman?"

From the back of the room came a voice, "He'd be in the Garden of Eden eating strawberries."

WONDERING

We have a strange and wonderful relationship. He's strange and I'm wonderful.

WOODEN LEG

Fred: There is a man outside with a wooden leg named Martin.

Jed: What is the name of his other leg?

WOOL

There was a man who owned many sheep and wanted to take them over a river that was frozen over, but the woman who owned the river said "No." So he promised to marry her, and that's how he pulled the wool over her ice.

WORRY

Red: I'd give a thousand dollars to anyone who would do my worrying for me.

Ted: You're on. Where's the thousand?
Red: That's your first worry.

WORSE NEWS

Bad news: Your wife was captured by cannibals.
Worse news: They have already eaten.

WRECKED

Pretty young girl to friend: "Not only has Jack broken my heart and wrecked my whole life, but he has spoiled my entire evening!"

WRONG AGAIN

Husband: We have been married five years and haven't agreed on a thing.
Wife: You're wrong again. It has been six years.

YAWN

It is always dullest just before the yawn.

*　　*　　*

My friend, have you heard of the town of Yawn, on the banks of the river Slow, where blooms the Waitawhile flower fair, where the Sometimeorother scents the air, and the Softgoeasys grow?

It lies in the valley of Whatstheuse, in the province of Letherslide; that tired feeling is native

there—it's the home of the listless Idon'tcare,
where the Putitoffs abide.

YOU SAID IT

Teacher: What do you call a person who keeps
on talking when people are no longer interested?
Student: A teacher.

YOU SURE TOLD THEM

There was a certain energetic young preacher
who had a thriving country church. He was always
prodding his people to do greater things for God.
He spent much time in preparation of his sermons.
There was a deacon in his congregation who did
little and seemed to care less. It caused the young
preacher much concern. On several occasions the
preacher would tell him exactly what he thought.
The old deacon never caught the point—he always
thought the preacher was referring to someone else.
One Sunday, the preacher made it plainer as to
whom he was talking. Following the service the
deacon said, "Preacher, you sure told them today."

The next sermon was still more pointed than
ever. Again the deacon said, "Preacher, you sure
told them today."

The next Sunday it rained so hard that no one
was at the church except this one deacon. The
preacher thought that the deacon would now know
about whom he was talking. The sermon went

straight to the deacon, who was the only one in the congregation. Following the service, the deacon walked up to the preacher and said, "Preacher, you sure told them if they had been here."

YOU'LL GET A BOOT OUT OF THIS

A psychiatrist was trying to comfort a new patient who was terribly upset. "You see, Doc," the patient explained, "my problem is that I like shoes much better than I like boots."

"Why, that's no problem," answered the doctor. "Most people like shoes better than boots."

The patient was elated, "That's neat, Doc. How do you like them, fried or scrambled?"

YOUNG WOMAN

The seven ages of a woman are baby, child, girl, young woman, young woman, young woman, and poised social leader.

ZIP YOUR LIP

Bill: Did you ever see a company of women silent?

Mike: Yes—when the chairman asked the oldest lady to speak first.

ZIPPER

Q. How do you make an elephant fly?

A. Well, first you take a grea-a-t big zipper...

Index

294

Other Books by Bob Phillips

WORLD'S GREATEST COLLECTION OF
CLEAN JOKES

THE RETURN OF THE GOOD
CLEAN JOKES

THE WORLD'S GREATEST COLLECTION
OF HEAVENLY HUMOR

THE WORLD'S GREATEST COLLECTION OF
RIDDLES AND DAFFY DEFINITIONS

THE WORLD'S GREATEST COLLECTION OF
KNOCK, KNOCK JOKES AND
TONGUE TWISTERS

THE BEST OF THE GOOD CLEAN JOKES

WIT AND WISDOM

HUMOR IS TREMENDOUS

THE ALL-NEW CLEAN JOKE BOOK

GOOD CLEAN JOKES FOR KIDS

THE ENCYCLOPEDIA OF
GOOD CLEAN JOKES

ULTIMATE GOOD CLEAN JOKES
FOR KIDS

AWESOME GOOD CLEAN JOKES
FOR KIDS

MORE AWESOME GOOD CLEAN JOKES
FOR KIDS

WACKY GOOD CLEAN JOKES FOR KIDS

NUTTY GOOD CLEAN JOKES FOR KIDS

LOONY GOOD CLEAN JOKES FOR KIDS

CRAZY GOOD CLEAN JOKES FOR KIDS

GOOFY GOOD CLEAN JOKES FOR KIDS

BIBLE BRAINTEASERS

THE GREAT BIBLE CHALLENGE

THE AWESOME BOOK OF
BIBLE TRIVIA

HOW CAN I BE SURE?

ANGER IS A CHOICE

REDI-REFERENCE

REDI-REFERENCE DAILY
BIBLE READING PLAN

THE DELICATE ART OF DANCING
WITH PORCUPINES

GOD'S HAND OVER HUME

PRAISE IS A THREE-LETTERED
WORD—JOY

FRIENDSHIP, LOVE & LAUGHTER

PHILLIPS' BOOK OF GREAT QUOTES &
FUNNY SAYINGS

THE ALL-AMERICAN QUOTE BOOK

BIBLE OLYMPICS

BIG BOOK—THE BIBLE—QUESTIONS
AND ANSWERS

THE UNOFFICIAL LIBERAL JOKE BOOK

WHAT TO DO UNTIL THE
PSYCHIATRIST COMES

For information on how to purchase any of the above books, contact
your local bookstore or send a self-addressed stamped envelope to:
Family Services
P.O. Box 9363
Fresno, CA 93702

Dear Reader:

We would appreciate hearing from you regarding this Harvest House nonfiction book. It will enable us to continue to give you the best in Christian publishing.

1. What most influenced you to purchase *The Best of the Good Clean Jokes*?
   - ☐ Author
   - ☐ Subject matter
   - ☐ Backcover copy
   - ☐ Recommendations
   - ☐ Cover/Title
   - ☐ _____

2. Where did you purchase this book?
   - ☐ Christian bookstore
   - ☐ General bookstore
   - ☐ Other
   - ☐ Grocery store
   - ☐ Department store

3. Your overall rating of this book:
   ☐ Excellent ☐ Very good ☐ Good ☐ Fair ☐ Poor

4. How likely would you be to purchase other books by this author?
   - ☐ Very likely
   - ☐ Somewhat likely
   - ☐ Not very likely
   - ☐ Not at all

5. What types of books most interest you?
   (check all that apply)
   - ☐ Women's Books
   - ☐ Marriage Books
   - ☐ Current Issues
   - ☐ Christian Living
   - ☐ Bible Studies
   - ☐ Fiction
   - ☐ Biographies
   - ☐ Children's Books
   - ☐ Youth Books
   - ☐ Other _____

6. Please check the box next to your age group.
   - ☐ Under 18
   - ☐ 18-24
   - ☐ 25-34
   - ☐ 35-44
   - ☐ 45-54
   - ☐ 55 and over

Mail to: Editorial Director
Harvest House Publishers
1075 Arrowsmith
Eugene, OR 97402

Name _____

Address _____

City _____ State _____ Zip _____